A Childhood in
CARNFORTH

1915   1925

by
Marion Russell

Published by Lundarien Press, UK

ISBN 978-1-910816-73-8

For more info and other books in this series:
www.lundarienpress.com

OTHER BOOKS IN THE

A HISTORY OF CARNFORTH SERIES

1. How Carnforth Grew - a simple outline to 1900AD

2. How Carnforth Steamed into the 20th Century

CONTENTS

Introduction   7

1915   10

1916   23

1917   35

1918   45

1919   54

1920   69

1921   91

1922   106

1923   133

1924   159

1925   192

Acknowledgements   233

INTRODUCTION

Recently I was looking through a large, beautifully-illustrated book about Lancashire and, of course, the first thing I searched for was a reference to Carnforth. What I read did not please me!

In a very long, complicated and poorly-constructed sentence, with so many phrases that one got lost along the way, the author wrote of where one might like to go after leaving Morecambe, "which as sea-side towns go may be described as Blackpool-Type."

One could choose between small, peaceful resorts like Silverdale, the Yealands, Arnside and Grange-over-Sands, "some no more than villages, but all individually interesting after one has shut one's eyes to Carnforth, a railway town which is even less interesting than the average railway town."

What a disparaging remark to make about our hometown!

Travelling about with closed eyes is not only highly dangerous, it in no way qualifies a person to give correct descriptions of any localities.

Had the author visited Carnforth with eyes open and brains switched on, he would have met welcoming, friendly folk and seen our grey buildings, some with gracefully-rounded corners and some with interesting tales of the past to tell people with ears to hear.

It used to be said that, if anyone kicked a person in Carnforth, half the townspeople would limp. Let an outsider make a derogatory remark about Carnforth and all the kicking legs in town would be activated!

When my contemporaries and I were little children, as far as we were aware, Carnforth was the hub of the universe. When I was old enough to study a map, it came as a great shock to me to find that Carnforth was not marked - not even with the tiniest of dots!

During our childhood, the World of Technology was rapidly developing, but amazing inventions which began to change people's lives took a considerable time to reach Carnforth. Apart from seeing the swift growth of motorised traffic, our young lives differed little from those of our parents.

Nowadays, whenever a group of us "old 'uns" gets together, it isn't long before the conversation turns to the good old days of our childhood. Tongues wag happily as we journey back along Memory Lane and we often hear the remark, "Someone ought to write it down!" Here is my attempt to do just that. I have tried, in snippet-form and chronological order, to link together my childhood memories alongside important events in the big outside world.

Good Wishes to all Carnforthians, (especially the "old 'uns").

Marion Russell. 2 Morningside.
20th November, 1999.

Station Buildings, Post Office (top left) next, Conservative Club (flag at half-mast), Crewdson's Chip Shop (lower right).

1915

I was born on June 10th - an event which was of no importance to anyone apart from my parents and their immediate families - and my birth-place was 13 Hill Street, Carnforth.

Our small two-up-two-down home had been rented from Riggs the Builders and Contractors by my parents Thomas Jackson Wilkinson, age 29, and Annie (née Barnham) age 27, after their marriage at Christ Church in 1914. I arrived in a war-torn world when national disasters were causing upheaval in the lives of millions of people.

When Britain had declared war on Germany on August 4th 1914, crowds in the cities had cheered at hearing the news. Patriotic young men, eager for excitement and adventure, had rushed to enlist in the Forces, and amongst them had been some of Carnforth's bright young sparks. They were all hoping to be sent overseas as soon as possible, because it was firmly believed that the war would be over before Christmas, with Britain and her Allies as victors.

By August 19th, a British Expeditionary Force of 70,000 men had landed in France, but they had little or no knowledge of what war really meant. 1915 brought the dreadful reality. Our country found itself embroiled in a dangerous conflict with the big, powerful enemy, and in January the future looked very frightening.

Warfare had started at sea and one of our powerful naval ships, HMS Formidable, was sunk in the North Sea. Germany had begun its plan to destroy the British economy by blockading our shores and depriving us of food and essential supplies. That month, 3 merchant ships were sunk in the Irish Sea by submarines, and people in our locality feared that Barrow-in-Furness, across Morecambe Bay, might be in some danger.

A sinister new development in the waging of war then made its appearance: a Zeppelin, a large dirigible airship, flew over the shores of Norfolk and rained death from the sky on unsuspecting towns. Civilian deaths numbered 20, and 40 people were seriously injured. "Zeppelins" now became the Bogey-Man word in Carnforth, scaring adults and children alike. A British citizen, named Hiram Maxim, had devised an incendiary bullet, which could ignite the gases in a Zeppelin. Carnforth people hoped that the bullet would save our Western coast from those airborne monsters.

The British Army now stood at 720,000, but the outlook was black indeed. As the year progressed, each month brought terrible disasters. Carnforth families, whose men were in the war zone near Ypres, were very disturbed when they read in the newspapers that swirling, greenish-yellow vapour had drifted into British trenches from enemy lines: Chlorine Gas! What Horror! The German troops had then attacked wearing gas-proof helmets.

A DISASTROUS DAY

The railway companies here in Carnforth had a club for their employees at the post-office-end of Platform 1. The building, an extension built at right-angles to the station frontage, had a reading room where men also played cards and dominoes, and a large room containing 2 fine billiard tables.

Dreadful news set tongues wagging there on May 7th. The railwaymen were distressed to learn that 2 torpedoes from an enemy submarine had sunk the huge Cunard passenger liner, THE LUSITANIA, off the Irish coast. It had sailed from New York across the Atlantic Ocean, and was steaming towards Liverpool. Hundreds of people had been drowned, including some very rich and important American citizens.

"Will this terrible event bring America into the war on our side?" wondered the men at the club. They hoped so, because Britain was sorely in need of all the help she could get.

Established in 1864, the Iron Works had declined in the early part of the 20th century. The manufacture of steel had ceased, and the use of locally-mined phosphorus-free haematite iron-ore, which had been of great benefit in the early days, had gradually become of less and less importance. The Works had faced fierce competition from rivals. Trade had gone into recession and many men had lost their jobs. Not all the unemployed men had been able to find work, either on our flourishing local railway or in any of the gravel-pits around our district. Consequently there had been a considerable amount of poverty in Carnforth.

View from the hill above the A6 (left) Pond Street and Pond Terrace overlooking the Iron Works' pond (cooling reservoir), Millhead and Warton Crag (right)

The outbreak of war stimulated a boom in Britain's heavy industries, and that brought a temporary boost to our Iron Works. Nevertheless, some men preferred to enlist in the Forces rather than return to their old jobs, which gave no promise of long-term employment.

THE LOCAL SHOOTING RANGE

The army had taken over a large area of flat, marshy land between Cragbank and the shore, to be used as a Shooting Range. The targets, placed on top of raised mounds of earth, were visible from Shore Lane. A path across the land had always been used as a shortcut to the shore, but red flags were now flown to warn the public not to enter the danger-zone as a shooting practice might be taking place.

10th Scottish Battalion Kings (Liverpool) who were billeted in Carnforth for shooting practice in 1914.

To gain experience with their rifles, groups of soldiers from a Liverpool Scottish regiment were brought by train to Carnforth for a stay of 3 weeks. People were asked to offer their homes as billets, and my grand-parents, William and Mary Barnham of 39 Highfield Terrace, were amongst those who volunteered. They had a spare bedroom, because only my young aunts, Ella and Bertha, were still living at home.

Handsome soldiers in swinging kilts looked irresistibly glamorous to many local young maidens, and romance blossomed for some!

RELAXATION FROM THE WORRIES OF WAR

A) SPORT

Sporting events provided recreation for many Carnforth men. Those who spent happy hours on the Cricket Field, situated behind Hewthwaite Terrace, were sad when they heard of the death of Doctor W G Grace, cricket's greatest figure-head and the game's finest exponent.

B) DRINK

After a hard day's work men looked forward to "Goin' tut Pub" - The Cross Keys, The Queen's Hotel, The Carnforth Inn, The Traveller's Rest or The Station Hotel (sawdust end only, of course). Before they set off, they were warned by their womenfolk that they must not say to their pals, "What's thine mate?" Treating was out! The Government had decided that excessive drinking was detrimentally affecting Britain's War Effort and, as a deterrent, a fine of £100 or 6 months in jail had been imposed for offenders. The organisers of the Band of Hope rejoiced at this news!

THE PICTURES

A new and wonderful form of entertainment had reached our town at last: moving pictures! The film-shows were put on in the Victoria Hall, which could accommodate 200 people and was part of the prestigious Station Hotel.

Seated on rows of hard wooden forms in front of a

'silver' screen, showing jerky, flickering films, Carnforth's people were transported in imagination from their drab, workday lives into the fabulous world of glamorous film stars. Favourites were Mary Pickford, Douglas Fairbanks, Charlie Chaplin and Fatty Arbuckle.

Before each performance, queues formed on the pavement at the door in Lower New Street, which was the entrance to the hall, at the foot of an indoor flight of stairs. My mother was sometimes in the waiting crowd holding me, a tiny baby, wrapped warmly in a big, white shawl. My father was a railway fireman, and shift-work meant that he was on duty some evenings. *[Babysitters hadn't been invented]*.

My Wilkinson grandparents, who lived at 38 Grosvenor Place, were very strict Wesleyans and thought it disgraceful that a babe, still in 'long clothes', should be taken to the pictures, which they considered to be a wicked form of entertainment (along with whist-drives and dances).

FASHIONABLE BABYWEAR

Homes were heated only by a coal fire in the living room so, during the winter, they were cold and draughty, and it was necessary for all the members of the family, including the baby, to wear several layers of garments to keep them comfortable.

My mother was the proud owner of a Jones Sewing

Machine with a box-lid, and she could treadle away with great confidence, having gained valuable experience at Morphy's Sewing Mill in Riggs' Yard at the end of Oxford Street. She made all my baby clothes, starting with a cotton singlet. Over that was a sleeveless 'Barrow-Coat', made of warm flannel, which was fastened round the body with tapes. Next came a long, cotton under-gown and, on top of that, a beautiful long gown, probably made of broderie anglaise and elaborately tucked. A lace-edged bonnet of the same material - white of course - completed the outfit, and the 'bundle of baby' was then enveloped in a big white shawl. Nappies were pieces of scrap material from old sheets, pillowcases etc. machine-sewn into neat squares.

It was quite an occasion when, a few months later, I was 'shortened' - my clothes, not my body!

After they were shortened, all babies wore dresses, so it was difficult to distinguish girls from boys at the toddler stage. The age at which little boys got 'britched' (put into breeches) depended upon their fond mothers.

Neighbours got quite a shock down Carnforth's Lake District (the Pond Street, Pond Terrace, Ramsden Street, Hunter Street area), when a 3-year-old girl-child, with long golden ringlets, changed into a betrousered little boy with closely cropped hair. His fed-up father had taken him to Adamson's Barbers' shop for a short back and sides!

MY CHRISTENING

I was Christened at Carnforth Christ Church by the Reverend Mercer, when I was 6 weeks old.

Now, a baby should most surely be the star at its Christening, but I was completely outshone at mine, even though I was wearing a beautiful robe lovingly sewn by my mother.

All the "Oos!" and "Ahs!" were bestowed on a fine, eight-month old baby boy, beaming at everybody and bouncing about in the arms of his proud father, a sailor in uniform, home on leave. That baby was named Arthur Swithenbank.

WHITE WASHING

Our churches frequently held White Sales, so named because many articles in common usage were made of white material: bed linen, tableware, towels, nighties, underwear, antimacassars, handkerchiefs, duchess sets, d'oyleys, etc.

"Use Robin Starch on Wash Day" said the advertisements on the wooden placards at the bottom of Market Street and Hawk Street.

They were pasted there by the Carnforth and District Billposting Company (sole proprietor W J Weeks, 38 Market Street).

Into an enamel bowl on wash-day, housewives

placed a tablespoonful of short, white sticks of starch which they crushed into a powder with the back of a spoon.

Uncle Arthur Barnham on spare land behind Market Street (site of the Health Centre and Booth's car park). Auntie Maggie is pegging out the washing after a busy washing day.

A little cold water was added for mixing before boiling water was poured in.

Ancient Egyptians were the 1st to discover that starch would make fabrics stiffer. It was made from wheat, sago or potatoes, and contained borax for a glossy finish.

Boiling articles, starting and then blue-ing them with 'dolly-blue', helped Carnforth women to obtain the colour and crispness of snow which they wanted for their Whites.

The ultimate disgrace for any local lady would be if someone said, "Eh! Aster sin 'er wershin' on t'line? It's as grey as t'owd woman's dish-clout!"

[Aster would appear to be a contraction of the question "Hast thou?"]

VACCINATION

Because of the war, large numbers of troops and refugees were being moved around the world as never before. This resulted in diseases being spread at an alarming rate from country to country. The fear of catching smallpox was almost causing a panic in the United Kingdom so, in an attempt to halt it, our Government decreed that all babies must be vaccinated.

Dr Jackson was the local Medical Officer of Health and, in due course, my mother was informed that I must be taken to his surgery for vaccination.

She disagreed with the whole procedure, and promptly returned home and washed the vaccine off my arm. Because of this, the treatment did not 'take' and I did not develop large scars in the formation of 4 dots on a domino as did other babies. Nor did I catch smallpox!

[In after years, when sleeveless dresses became fashionable, young ladies hated the disfigurement on their left arms]

WORRYING WAR NEWS

As the months passed by, the war was never far from anyone's thoughts and, in October, the sobering news was that a million Britons were on the Western front and there were 510,230 casualties.

View from Thwaite canal bridge, looking towards Carnforth.
Wooded area on the left is now Longfield Drive

The German blockade was beginning to cause a shortage of goods imported from overseas. To make sure that they would have all they needed for their Christmas puddings, mince pies and cakes, the members of Carnforth Co-operative Society went early in December to put in their order forms at the big grocery store, entered by 2 door-ways in New Street.

At the top counter, assistants were kept busy weighing-up sugar, dried fruit, rice etc. on large brass scales, and packing them neatly in blue paper bags. A line of shiny, brass weights stood in order from the tiny ounce to the heavy 7 lbs (1/2 stone).

Customers' orders were packed in discarded wooden margarine boxes, and delivered to their doorsteps by horse-and-cart.

When that patient animal came down Hill Street, it knew at which house to stand whilst the carter was unloading the boxes, and was pleased when rewarded by a grateful customer with a carrot or a sugar-lump.

A SAD CHRISTMAS

During the Festive Season, the absence of loved ones brought sorrow and anxiety to the hearts of many families, especially because the lives of those dear ones were in grave danger. When gathered around pianos in parlours up Haws Hill, Edward Street, New Street, Annas Bank, etc. etc., families sang patriotic songs as well as the familiar, beloved carols. Many young ladies did not feel like Packing-Up Their Troubles in anyone's Old Kit-Bag, because it was rumoured that, very soon, all single men would have to join the Forces, whether they wanted to or not!

Quite a number of weddings were hastily planned.

1916

It had become the custom for many Carnforthians to assemble late each New Year's Eve on the untidy-looking piece of spare land at the bottom of Market Street. There they waited for all the railway engines in the busy marshalling-yard to shrill their whistles and herald in the New Year.

1916 was not welcomed in with the usual cheers. As hands were linked and 'Auld Lang Syne' was sung, worried thoughts were turned to our brave lads entrenched in foreign lands overseas, far from their loving homes in Carnforth. The outlook was dark and threatening.

CONSCRIPTION

Because the list of casualties was increasing at an alarming rate each day, the Forces were in desperate need of more men to replace those brave volunteers who were falling in battle.

Half a million fit, unmarried men were deemed to be shirking their duty by not enlisting, and the Government had reluctantly come to the decision that Conscription would have to be introduced for the first time in British history.

In January, however, the Labour Party Conference voted heavily against the idea, but their dissension had no effect on the outcome and, in March, the Military Service Act came into force.

This did not have as great an effect in Carnforth as it did in many places, because so many men worked on the railway, and their jobs were classed as reserved occupations.

Trains carrying troops, munitions and essential supplies had to be kept on the move, and our town echoed to the strident whistles of speeding steam engines and the loud rattle of express trains as they sped along and north-south main line.

THE BLOCKADE

The blockade of our shores by the mighty German fleet and its deadly submarines was causing the Government such grave concern that 'A Ministry of Blockade' was set up. It had to eliminate the import of non-essential goods and ensure the supply of food was maintained.

The import of paper, tobacco, spirits, motors and pianos was banned for the duration of the war. That news caused a lot of grumbling among the regulars at the Cross Keys public house on Kellet Road.

"Banning moters and pianners don't worry me," grizzled Owd Fred, "but they 'as it in fer us knocking off us baccy, booze and papers!"

The Government's appeal for people not to use their motor cars for pleasure was hardly necessary in Carnforth! One of the first locally-owned cars to be seen round our streets was a Morris, owned by the Lee-Bookers of Whittington - a tea-planting family.

The son married Nellie Jackson, our Dr Jackson's daughter, and the couple had two little girls known, to one and all, by the surprising names of Chitty and Bubbles.

RELEASE OF SERVANTS

In February, the Government issued an edict requiring well-off families to shut-up part of their homes, close down greenhouses, and have simpler meals so as to release male and female servants for more useful purposes.

Inside its boundaries, Carnforth did not have any large country houses to which the regulation would apply. Mainly, the population was made up of working-class people, who lived in our streets and terraces.

There were, however, some better-off families who occupied more imposing, detached houses, and some of them employed servants - e.g. Robin Hill (Market Street) Red Court, Redcar House, The Lodge, The Launds (Lancaster Road) Hall Gowan, Carnforth House, Meresbeck, Plane Tree House etc. (North Road) The Hollies, Thwaite House (Cragbank).

DAY-LIGHT SAVING PLAN

Farmer Ireland of Cockle Hall Farm supplied Hill Street folk with their milk - warm, creamy and frothy - direct from cow to doorstep. Early each morning, pint or quart jugs were put out, with an old cup or plate on top to protect the milk from creepy-crawlies, flying insects, cats with lapping tongues and doggies liable to lift a back leg.

As he stopped outside Number 13 and proceeded to use a measure to dip out milk from the churn at the back of his float, the farmer had a very cross face one morning in May.

"Mi cows are all confused and upset," he grumbled. "They're moo-ing for an hour at the field gates waiting to come in and be milked. They don't understand what the Government's playing at, making everybody put their clocks forward an hour."

The idea was that fuel would be saved by introducing British Summer Time, and people could work an extra hour before Lighting-up Time.

AIR RAIDS

Zeppelins became a real menace. There were raids on 8 counties and, one night, 13 of the monsters raided London.

Over the Thames Estuary one Spring morning, a brave young New Zealander in the Royal Flying Corps, who had only gained his wings 3 weeks previously, flew his plane to machine-gun range of a Zeppelin and shot it down.

So far, our area had been free from aerial attacks,

26

but any unusual noise in the night now caused Carnforth people to quake in their beds.

NAVAL WARFARE

Having enjoyed sailing paper boats along raging rainwater racing down the gutters of our streets, some local lads were considering becoming sailors when their call-up came. They had second thoughts in May, however, when news arrived of a terrible sea battle, the greatest in history. It had taken place at Jutland between the coasts of Norway and Denmark, when the powerful fleets of Britain and Germany fought in bitter conflict and hurled shells weighing a ton at each other from mighty Dreadnoughts. It was not clear which side was the winner. The German ships limped back to the shelter of their country's coastal waters, but the British Navy seemed to have lost more ships: 1 battleship, 1 battle cruiser, 5 destroyers and sadly 6,907 men.

A NEW WEAPON OF WAR

Railway engines and motor cars fascinated many Carnforth lads. They were very interested when they heard about the Allies' latest weapons of war: a huge, armoured motor vehicle, mounted with guns, which moved not on wheels but on caterpillar tracks. It had been built in strict secrecy under the codename T.A.N.K.

When the first raid of 30 Allied tanks rolled over the German lines, its scattered machine-gunners and crashed through enemy strong points. Within 2 hours, over 2000 German prisoners were taken.

"Germany is kaput!" groaned one of the captured enemy, but it wasn't … yet! And some of our wonderful tanks broke down.

Several of our school-boys decided that they would drive tanks, not railway engines, when they grew up.

[Sadly, one or two of them did!]

ANOTHER INVENTION

Our townspeople with enquiring minds had plenty to puzzle over. Medical Science announced the discovery of a procedure by which internal organs of the human body could be photographed: the X-ray.

Very few people here owned cameras to photograph the outsides of their friends and relations! They were not interested in the insides.

The lack of cameras, however, in no way meant an absence of photographs in Carnforth homes. Framed pictures were perched on all available places, large ornate albums were lovingly treasured, and in each room hung big photographs, suspended on cord from nails hammered into the walls - bearded grandfathers, grandmothers with stern expressions, beloved aunts and uncles and family groups taken at weddings or proudly arranged at back doors.

W R Taylor, Photographer, had a studio at 38 Lancaster Road. He charged from 3 shillings per dozen for photographs of postcard size and from £1 4s 0d per dozen for double cabinet size (8 in x 6 in).

In pride of place now went photographs of sons in uniform, away from home, fighting for Britain.

A HOME-CURE

One night when she was getting me ready to go into my cot, my mother was concerned because my chest sounded 'rattly and wheezy'.

Like all well-run families, ours had home-cures, passed on by word-of-mouth from one generation to another, for all common ailments.

For instance, to ease bad colds, the Barnhams advocated a supper of boiled onions topped with a big knob of butter. Then one had to sit with one's feet in a small tin bath of hot water, containing a tablespoonful of Colman's mustard. That drew the cold out of the head, you know!

Finally, before going to bed, one must drink a cup of hot milk, generously laced with rum. (Very enjoyable even if it didn't work as a cure!)

My mother knew that sore throats and congested chests responded well to an application of goose grease but, because she had none, she decided to use an alternative remedy suitable for a toddler. She wrapped a piece of fatty bacon round my throat and secured it in place with a warm, woolly scarf and a big safety pin.

Next morning she was delighted to see me sitting up, all bright and perky. The bacon had done its job ... but where was it? She couldn't find it anywhere. I'd eaten it! Taken internally, the remedy proved to be more effective than an external application.

Crowded canteen at Lancaster Munitions factory. Outdoor clothing hung along walls.

WOMEN AT WAR

As more and more men were called up for military service, women all over Britain began to sign up for war work. Their help to the war effort was immensely successful.

Troublesome Suffragettes, who had been imprisoned for assaulting policemen, were given

30

their freedom so that they could go and use their aggression against the Germans.

Some young Carnforth ladies travelled by train to Lancaster or Morecambe to work in munition factories. Others, who had been brought up on local farms or had been farm servants, were able to offer valuable service on the land.

The Government aimed to recruit 400,000 women to help till the fields and grow the food urgently needed by our nation. Elizabeth Battersby was among the local young ladies who joined the Women's Land Army, and Carnforth was proud when it was announced that she had been awarded a medal for stopping a run-away horse.

By November, 3 million British women were employed outside the home, but in Carnforth the saying, 'A woman's place is in the home', still applied to mothers, especially those who had large families.

They had the difficult task of providing cheap, nourishing meals for their husbands and children, and were very worried when the price of a large loaf at the Co-op Confectionery Department in New Street rose to the alarming price of 10d - only 24 loaves for £1!

POLITICS

"He's a grand fella!" declared the members of Carnforth's Liberal Party at their club-room at the top of Stanley Street *[a launderette at present].* They were welcoming the news that David Lloyd George, the Minister in Charge of Munitions, had been appointed by King George V to succeed Herbert Asquith as Prime Minister. The Tory leader, Bonar Law, had declined to take over.

The Carnforth Liberals were not at all sorry to learn that Winston Churchill, the First Lord of the Admiralty, had been dropped from the war cabinet.

THE NEWS

Before the war, people had looked forward to the delivery of their favourite daily newspapers, which kept them informed of what was going on in the world.

Paper-lads, delivering for our town's 2 busiest newsagents (William Weeks and Joseph Smith, numbers 38 and 23 Market Street, respectively), could be the bearers of sad news in 1916. Anxious eyes scanned the long, long lists of names of the 'Fallen'. By the end of a 3-month period there had been more than 350,000 British casualties.

The sight of the telegraph boy, riding his bicycle or walking along one of our streets with an ominous buff-coloured envelope in his hand, struck terror into people's hearts. At which door would he stop to deliver the telegram, conveying the tragic news from the War Office that a loved one had been killed in action, was grievously wounded or missing, presumed dead?

The number of young widows and fatherless children in Carnforth was rising at an alarming rate, and fond parents were distraught.

WINTER EVENINGS

Like most living-rooms in Carnforth, my home at 13 Hill Street had a rocking-chair at each side of the big iron range with its welcoming open coal-fire. Whilst reading the Daily Mail and smoking his pipe, Dad relaxed comfortably in his rocker, which had wooden arm-rests and a padded seat and back-rest.

Mother's chair did not have arm-rests because, like nearly all mothers, her free time was spent knitting, patching and darning. Her time to relax came when she sang lullabies and gently rocked me to sleep. Her favourite songs were: "You can't come and play in our yard" and "In the little shirt my mother made for me." *[I can still remember them!]*

CHRISTMAS-TIDE

For a number of years, Carnforth ladies had enjoyed going to meetings known as Sewing Bs, which were hives of industry for the production of articles which would sell at various church bazaars. A buzz of happy conversation accompanied the work.

This winter, instead of sewing nightdress-cases, crocheting d'oyleys or embroidering handkerchiefs, the women knitted khaki-coloured stockings, scarves, mittens and balaclava helmets. These were lovingly made up into parcels and sent off overseas to Carnforth lads with the British forces, who were suffering from the chill of continental weather, and feeling sad and homesick as they listened to the song, "Take me back to dear old Blighty."

Some entertainers have joined the war effort to boost the spirits of our 'Tommies' abroad, and shows were held along the British Front during brief respites from fighting. The most popular feature at such performances was the singalong.

Here in Carnforth, "Keep the home fires burning" was sung with fervour as families gathered to celebrate Christmas in the traditional way. Young wives and sweethearts pined for their absent loved ones as they joined in the singing of, "If you were the only girl in the world." Each one hoped most sincerely that she was her boy's only girl, and that some saucy Mademoiselle from Armentiers wasn't parlez-vous-ing with him!

BOXING DAY

In the Co-operative Hall, over the row of shops in New Street, the Congregational Sunday School put on a hugely successful concert of sketches, recitations, skipping drill and a cantata. *[This excellent entertainment started what was to become an annual event much enjoyed by Carnforth people.]*

1917

WAR LOANS

It was disclosed in the New Year that, to finance the war, it was costing our country the staggering sum of £5 million per day. David Lloyd George, the Prime Minister, and Andrew Bonar Law, the Chancellor of the Exchequer, launched a patriotic campaign to raise the money. Placards appeared on all the hoardings in Carnforth and throughout Britain, announcing: "You can help to win the war with 5 shillings (25p). Subscribe to the new war loan and save the lives of brave young men at the front. A safe and patriotic investment. Apply at your nearest Post Office." My parents, along with many, many Carnforthians, did just that.

TIGHTENING BELTS

The German blockade, by warships and submarines, was strangling Britain, and the Government asked people to use less of everything, especially flour. In one month, about 100 merchant ships had been sunk, so plans were made to sail ships in convoys, protected by warships.

The shortage of wheat became so serious that, on 4 consecutive Sundays in May, a proclamation from King George V was read in our Parish Church, and in churches throughout the land. His Majesty requested everyone to hold back on bread consumption and eat a quarter less than in peace-time. Our king would never ask his subjects to make sacrifices in which he was not prepared to share. The Royal household had been rationing itself since February.

Carnforth ladies became very ingenious at making thrifty, nourishing meals and ensuring that nothing was wasted.

THE CONGREGATIONAL CHURCH

Our highly esteemed Brass Band still heartened the town with its uplifting music during the dark days of war. A room was rented from the Congregational Church for practice purposes, and the 18 bandsmen promised to keep it tidy and put their instruments away.

The large school-room was let to B Company 13th Battalion of the Lancashire Volunteer Regiment on Mondays and Fridays for drill purposes. The church caretaker must have felt he deserved higher wages for all the extra work he was being called upon to do, and asked for a rise from 7 shillings (35p) to 10 shillings (50p) per week.

THE VOTE

"Does thy missis know owt about politics?" asked Tom, when he met Arthur outside the Conservative Club in Station Buildings. "'cause I read in t'Daily Herald this morning that all married wimmin ovver 30 is going t'git t'vote."

"I dunno," replied Arthur. "But if she dunt I'll larn 'er."

That seed, planted by those troublesome the Suffragettes years ago, had grown and blossomed at last!

WAR WORK

At Morphy's Sewing Mill, the market for fashion blouses and dresses decreased as the war went on and times got harder. Ella and Bertha Barnham, along with other young ladies, gave in their notices so that they could give more practical help to the war effort at Waring and Gillows factory in Lancaster.

There, they sewed fabric for aeroplane wings and painted them with strong-smelling 'dope'. They also made horse-rugs for cavalry regiments and mosquito nets for troops serving in hot countries.

Factory conditions were far from ideal! As there were no canteen facilities, the employees ate at their benches, a whistle signalling the beginning and end of meal-breaks. Tea, which was brewed from steam in the engine-room, was carried across the yard on large wooden trays.

Those teenage girls put in a 15-hour day, catching the 7.25am train each morning and returning on the 9.25pm at night. The long walk between the station and 39 Highfield Terrace added to the time spent away from home.

[My Auntie Bertha gave me this account when she was 90.]

TITLES

The thoughts of Carnforth people returned to Mrs German when they learnt that King George V had dropped his German titles: Saxe-Coberg Gotha. From now on, our Royal Family would be known as the House of Windsor, and the Battenberg branch would become Mountbattens.

Mrs German had moved from her tripe shop in Lower New Street to one opposite the Church on Lancaster Road. She had tried unsuccessfully to change her surname to Germaine, but some people still thought she was involved in enemy espionage.

It could be that their suspicions were misdirected. A well-known tradesmen, who was a highly respected member of our community, suddenly shut his shop in Market Street and vanished from the area. Rumour had it that he had turned out to be a German Spy!

[No names. No pack-drill!]

AIR RAIDS

Carnforth people stopped what they were doing and gazed skyward in wonderment whenever the zoom of an aeroplane was heard. Those mechanical birds were no novelty, however, to folk who lived in the East and South of England.

In June, it was reported that, for 15 minutes, the first bombing raid on London was carried out by 15 German aircraft. 100 people were killed and

400 injured. This was a sinister new role for aeroplanes which up to this time had been used for reconnaissance.

Some foolish Londoners had climbed onto roofs to catch a glimpse of the raiders. A number of M.P.s pressed for air-raid hooters or sirens to be installed, but the Government felt they would cause chaos and might be used by some people to take time off work. Policemen on bikes, with notices hanging round their necks saying "Take Cover!" would give warning of any future air-raids!

FOR VALOUR

In October, a wave of pride spread over Carnforth when it was learnt that Albert Halton, aged 24, one of our local soldiers, had been awarded the Victoria Cross. What an outstanding honour!

The bronze used for this decoration came from a Russian Canon captured after the fall of Sebastopol during the Crimean War (1854-56) and, although it is rather a plain medal, it is Britain's most highly-prized award. On one side is a likeness of Queen Victoria's head and on the reverse side just two words: For Valour.

Albert Halton lived with his parents, his sister Ethel and brother Walter at 19 Highfield Terrace, and the family were well known to The Barnhams at number 39. Albert was 5 years younger than my mother Annie (born 1888), but he most probably played out with her younger brothers Arthur and

Willie. She said he was just a lad like the others and gave no indication of the bravery he was later to display.

On leaving school, he went to work for a local contractor (probably Riggs) and, on August 15th 1915, he joined the 5th Battalion of the King's Own Royal Lancaster Regiment *[H.Q. at Bowerham Barracks, now St Martin's College].*

In October 1916, he was wounded on the Somme and, after recuperating in England, he was posted to the 1st Battalion K.O.R.L.R. He was awarded the V. C. for gallantry during an attack near Peolcappelle on October 12th, 1917.

The London Gazette published this citation: "For most conspicuous bravery in attack. After the objective had been reached, Private Halton rushed forward about 300 yards under very heavy rifle and shell fire and captured a machine-gun and its crew, which was causing many losses to our men. He then went out again and brought in about 12 prisoners, showing the greatest disregard of his own safety and setting a very fine example to those around him."

THE YANKS ARRIVED

"About time too!" said the chaps from Hope Terrace and the Cragbank area, who were having a drink at the Travellers' Rest when they heard that the Dough Boys - American soldiers - had fired their first shots in the war, and had joined our

Tommies in the muddy trenches of Flanders in October.

(The Americans had joined in the war in April, but had said at that time that they were not making fighter aircraft. The strength of their regular army was not big and it would take time to train additional troops. Crossing the Atlantic would be difficult, said the Yanks. It had been the end of June when their first troopships reached the French coast, where huge crowds had gathered to cheer them enthusiastically.)

EVACUATION

One moonlit night in October, when most folk had gone to bed, a terrific explosion, which could be heard as far away as Burnley, shook the ground in Carnforth. Pots and pans rattled and windows were shattered.

The immediate reaction was, "It's a Zeppelin raid!" and, still in their nighties and night-shirts, people dashed out into the street. On our main road, crowds of people were heading northward as if escaping from some danger, so Carnforthians felt they had to join in. No one knew what was happening!

Dashing back indoors, they tossed coats over nightwear, grabbed howling babies from cradles and put them in their perambulators along with family treasures. Then they joined the exodus which was heading mostly down Scotland Road.

My dad was 'on nights', so my mother carried me up to my grandparent's home in Highfield Terrace and joined the family group, which headed for Kellet Seeds (a wooded hill).

For miles crowds trudged wearily along into the countryside, and some lucky people were given refreshments at village church halls.

Eventually the news seeped through by word-of-mouth about the huge explosion and subsequent lesser ones. At White Lund, near Morecambe, an ammunition shed had blown up, and exploding shells threatened nearby storage huts. At the munitions factory, shells were filled with gunpowder and each night a heavy munitions train, which required 2 engines to pull it, left for one of the war-zone ports.

People from a wide area had been told to leave their homes and head for open country. As hundreds had left Morecambe, the bridge over the River Lune had become blocked with crowds converging on to it. In their frantic haste, some people had swum across the swollen river, and one man was reported to have drowned.

Dawn came and, as no more explosions were heard, tired people turned and set off back home, longing for their comfy feather beds. Our local evacuation was over, but the event was a topic of conversation for many years! All Hill Street had to show for it was the shattered shop window at the top of the street.

IN THE BLEAK MIDWINTER

Proudly on display on many Carnforth mantelpieces were postcards from soldiers with beautiful embroidered pictures of flags, flowers and birds. Sadly, as winter wore on, the cards brought distressing news of the dreadful conditions which our troops were having to endure in the war zones.

Ceaseless bombardment and remorseless rainstorms had turned fields, especially around Passchendaele, into a quagmire. The drainage system in Flanders was wrecked by bombs and rain. If a soldier slipped from the duck-boards, he could be sucked to his death in mud. There was a mounting list of missing men.

Wartime shortages were felt keenly at home as Christmas came round once again, but sacrifices were made so that parcels could be sent to the lads 'over there'. One item need not be included this year, a Christmas pudding. The War Office supplied one to all British troops in France.

Many Carnforth children only knew their daddies as photographs on sideboards, others only remembered him as a khaki-clad stranger, who occasionally stayed at their home on a week's leave from the trenches. Our railway station was the scene of many heart-breaking goodbyes.

The parlour-song at family-gatherings this Christmas was "Good-Bye-EE." (Don't sigh-ee.

Wipe that tear, baby dear, from your eye-ee.)

Many were the tears!

Carnforth Station. View is from Platform 1 before the addition of Platform 6. In the background can be seen the Iron Works chimney.

1918

The New Year's resolution for our townspeople was to keep to a strict diet, because the German blockade of our shores was causing an ever-increasing shortage of food. In January, the Government ordered restaurants and eating-houses not to serve meat on 2 days each week. The eating-houses of Carnforth were people's own homes, where meat on the menu every day was too expensive. Fish and 'rabbuts' bought from Jackie Blackburn's horse-and-cart 'mobile shop' were nourishing alternatives.

OUR POST OFFICE

Below the busy Post Office in Station Buildings which dealt with the counter-work, there was a large sorting-office with an entrance at the back of the buildings. During the night, trains brought mail-bags to Carnforth station, where Post Office workers loaded them onto trucks which they wheeled into the sorting office.

Mail for a wide country area was handled there. By local trains, or postmen on bicycles, letters and parcels were taken to the surrounding villages - Silverdale, the Kellets, Yealand, Bolton-le-Sands etc. - and as far away as Kirkby Lonsdale and Ingleton. Their mail was brought here on the return journeys and sorted ready for dispatch by train from our station to places all over the world.

By the Cragbank railway bridge was a contraption

from which our Post Office staff suspended a series of large sacks of mail which could be grabbed by passing expresses, and their contents sorted during journeys.

What people grumbled about in the year's budget was not just the raising of taxes, but the abolition of the Penny Post.

WOMEN WORKERS

Two million women in Britain were now employed outside the home, but the percentage of mothers having jobs was still low in Carnforth.

Women were having to take over the duties of men who were called-up and, by this time, our railway station was mainly staffed by women. The Owen family was well represented. Mr J Owen, the Station Master, had his daughter, Ruth, and his daughter-in-law, Sarah, working alongside him.

CARNFORTH MATTERS

1. Doctor Jackson walked along our streets with his Little Black Bag, well-stocked with new babies, as he went on his rounds of visiting patients in their homes. He jogged to neighbouring villages with his pony and trap. To spare themselves from big medical bills, some countryfolk were known to offer him a 'sack o' taties' or a freshly-plucked chicken as payment for his services.

2. Every home had an open coal fire, so the

hour at which one arose in a morning was indicated by the plumes of smoke ascending 'fray t' chimley'. There could be no breakfast cup o' tea until the fire was well alight. One railway chap down 'Grovner' (Grosvenor Place), who liked to rise with the lark, was often heard to remark in railway parlance, "I can't abide fowk wot ligs wakken i' thur beds. Slonks I calls 'em!"

3. The salesman, who sold fruit and vegetables from his cart, had a peg-leg which was a source of wonderment to the little children down Hill Street. One day, when I was 3, I lifted up his trouser-leg, tapped his wooden limb and asked with great concern, "Mamma, whatever is the matter with Mr Waghorne's leg?" Sometimes, when he and his horse were in a good mood, he gave children a ride down the street on his cart. What excitement!

4. Children who had reached their 13th birthday at the end of the educational year, in March, could not leave school as they had hoped. The Government had raised the school-leaving age to 14 years to ensure that children had an adequate education. Many scholars at the Church of England School on Lancaster Road and the Council School on Lower North Road were not at all pleased.

5. Children, whose dads were fighting in the

war, thought things were getting into a dreadful state when their Granddads got their calling-up papers. A new Military Service Bill had raised the maximum conscription age to 50!

6. In April, the Royal Flying Corps and the Royal Naval Air Service merged and became the Royal Air Force. The lads up Hall Street and along Russell Road etc. could now stretch out their arms and zoom along the streets as RAF fighter pilots. Some boys even liked pretending to be that dreaded enemy pilot, Von Richthofen, in his red plane. When news came that he had been shot from the skies and killed, the lads felt quite sad. The 'Red Baron' had been an exciting airman, even though he was a super 'baddy' and had shot down 80 Allied aircraft.

7. Carnforth people were quite unimpressed when they read that, in America, a pop-up machine for toasting bread had been invented. It worked by electricity. What was electricity? Most homes in our town had a special, long-handled fork hanging on the wall near the fire-place, and making toast was a pleasant job.

8. The Government ordered the rationing of coal, gas and electricity, and said that restaurants must close at 10pm and theatres at 10.30. Only the control of coal

consumption applied in Carnforth, and its cost ensured that it was used sparingly.

9. Harassed mothers down Hill Street had a good tip for keeping toddlers from under their feet on busy washing days: pop them into a spare dolly-tub. (Not containing water of course!) The women, wearing their hessian 'pinnies', could then get on with their dollying, boiling, mangling, scrubbing hubby's "ovveralls an' k-eye-tles", pegging-out on the clothes line etc. etc.

   [Those jackets and overalls, made of strong, denim-type material, were the uniforms of foot plate men on the railway. No one ever dreamt that half a century later they would become high fashion, suitable for all social occasions, including weddings and funerals!]

10. At the end of all events in our town, we stood to attention and sang "God Save The King" with patriotic pride. We respected King George V because he was a good sovereign, and we shared his sorrow at the dreadful news that his foreign relative Czar Nicholas II of Russia, and all his royal family, had been murdered by the Bolsheviks, who had taken over control of the country. Not only were the Royal Romanovs shot and bayoneted to death, but also the family's doctor, valet, cook, parlour maid and dog.

AN UNPOPULAR NAME

Bertha was not being chosen as a name for baby girls getting christened by the Reverend Mercer at our parish church. Females who already had the name were not pleased when a horrific new gun was called "Big Bertha." It was named after the wife if its German manufacturer, Gustav Krupps, and could fire on Paris from 65 miles away. That gun was very loud, unwieldy and inaccurate at targeting. Not a pleasant namesake!

Talking of names, I was really indignant when I heard that the Makinson family, lower down our street, had named their new baby Marion. Marion? That was surely my very own, personal name, invented especially for me. The cheek of it! That child had better never invade my territory in the middle area of Hill Street!

THE WAR DRAGGED ON

As summer approached, news from our men over there was very upsetting. In an effort to achieve victory before the arrival of more American forces, 300,000 German troops were hammering the Allied lines in France. The British line, in one sector, was shattered and it seemed that the Germans were about to realise their aim to roll our troops back to the Channel. 80,000 prisoners were taken. Earl Haig, the British Commander-in-Chief, issued the order that every position must be held to the last man. It meant backs to the wall. No retreating! In one 3-week period the Allies lost

400,000 men. "Will this awful war never end?" asked worried wives, mothers and sweethearts in Carnforth.

Then, for nearly the whole month of July, there was a lull in the fighting due to a very severe epidemic of influenza, which attacked both Allied and German forces. During that time the tide turned for the Allies because American troops were arriving in France at the rate of 300,000 per month.

THE END AT LAST

August 8th was a black day for the Germans. Near Amiens, 20 Allied divisions, with planes and tanks, went into action: British, American, Canadian, Australian and French troops. The Germans were pushed back and batches of prisoners were brought back in a steady stream, fed up with war and glad to surrender.

On September 30th, President Wilson announced in Washington that the Allies were sweeping all before them along the whole Western Front. Hurrah! Hurrah! The end came suddenly in October, whilst a new offensive was being planned.

Loud whistles echoed all over Carnforth at 11.00am on the 11th day of the 11th month. They were the signal of victory, sounded by all the railway engines in the marshalling yards and the 3 locomotive sheds. People rushed out into the streets, laughing and cheering at the wonderful news that the Great War was over at last, and we had won!

Guns became silent on the battlefields of Europe as German Generals signed an armistice in a railway carriage in the Forest of Compiègne, and admitted defeat.

All over the country next day, there was public revelry and rejoicing. Factories were shut and crowds massed in the streets, waving flags and letting off fireworks. In London, Big Ben chimed the hours again.

On November 19th, Germany became a republic when our King's wicked cousin, Kaiser Wilhelm II, abdicated. Because he was a very tall monarch, Carnforth people had disparagingly referred to him as 'Little Willie'.

PEACE ON EARTH

At the end of November, the German Fleet surrendered. Scores of vessels - battleships, cruisers and destroyers - lay at anchor in the Firth of Forth under the eye of the British Navy. 39 U-boats sailed to Harwich to give themselves up.

Christmas brought festive joy for the Carnforth families, whose men would be home 'ere long - some from the battlefields and some among the 1 million prisoners of war released by the Germans.

Christmas, however, meant grief and sorrow for other families, who would not see their loved ones ever again. Never in History had there been anything like the Great War. 10 million people had died worldwide.

Carnforth had very sadly lost 47 men and many more had been wounded.

1919

To the sound of church bells and engine whistles, a Peaceful New Year was welcomed in by a cheerful group of Carnforthians assembled on the Market Ground.

Now that the war was over, everyday life was resumed in our town. The lads, who had been called-up into the Forces, returned as men, and looked around for the jobs and homes fit for heroes which had been promised to them.

For the timebeing, they returned to the homes of their parents and that caused over-crowding.

Building-work had stopped during the war so now there was much to be done. The Council selected a site in Cote Flat Field, behind Annas Bank in Kellet Road, for the eventual erection of 40 houses. Prince Avenue was to be the first project and would lay the foundation for a large housing estate.

The boost in trade which the war had given to the Iron Works was over. Trade was dropping off and there was much unemployment among the men who had worked there.

There was industrial discontent throughout Britain and, in January, 200,000 workers were on strike. Mounted police were needed to break up demonstrations in some large towns.

A STRANGE ACHIEVEMENT

Carnforth folk were puzzled when they read in their newspapers that a professor at Manchester University had discovered how to split the atom. What did that mean? How could that have any effect on their lives? Perhaps they would find out someday in the future. *[They did!]*

TRANSPORT DEVELOPMENT

Very few Carnforthians had had the thrill of riding in a car, and certainly none of them had flown across the sky in an aeroplane. Would anyone here ever do such a remarkable thing?

They were very interested to learn in February that some military personnel had been flown from London to Paris in 3 ½ hours at the amazing speed of 97 miles per hour. Experts hoped that that historic flight would lead the way to a passenger service, once civil flying was resumed. In March, the huge British dirigible, R34, set off on a trial flight with enough fuel to journey to America and back.

During the same month, it was reported that the Government was in favour of a Channel tunnel connecting England and France. Of all the stupid ideas! Derisive laughter rang around the country.

A KILLER DISEASE

The virulent strain of Spanish influenza, which had swept around the world killing millions of people, finally reached Britain. An ominous statistic revealed in March that more deaths than births were recorded.

Our population, weakened by the strains and deprivations of war, had little resistance to the epidemic. Attempts to develop a vaccine to combat the disease had failed, and doctors predicted that more people could die of flu than were killed in the war.

Our 2 doctors in Carnforth could not cope with the severity of the epidemic: Dr Jackson at his surgery in Market Street and Dr Moss at 72 Lancaster Road, near the short parade of shops facing the entry to Oxford Street.

Whole families succumbed to the illness, and it was then that Carnforth folk benefited from the good neighbourliness which had always abounded in our town. They cared for each other's children, and nursing the sick became a communal effort. Quart-jugs full of beef-tea and pint-pots of nourishing barley-water or oatmeal gruel were carried carefully from door to door. Calves' foot jelly was a good builder-upper, but rather expensive.

Whilst my parents were ill, 3 lovely, motherly neighbours looked after me: Mrs Rainford, Mrs Howie and Mrs Fred Murray. One Friday evening, I sat very happily at one end of the Howie's large tin bath, in front of a glowing coal fire in the living-room, whilst their many young ones were washed at the other end. It didn't worry me at all that the water gradually turned soupy and grey.

STARTING SCHOOL

I was 4 years old and my mother decided that I was ready for school. *[And was she glad?]* One of Mrs Howie's big girls took my hand and led me off on my educational adventure. There was not far to go. The big Church of England School on Lancaster Road, which both my parents had attended, was visible from our doorstep.

We crossed the Girls' playground, having gone through a gate in the School lane, and entered the Infant Department on the lower floor by the doorway opposite. For some reason or other, the baby class was not in the charge of a teacher but of a governess named Miss Timperly.

A dolls' house and a sand-tray are only vaguely recalled. Pot hooks are what I remember! Pot-hooks sloping up from bottom-left to top-right, and pot hooks sloping down from top-left to bottom-right, all painstakingly formed between horizontal lines on a slate, with a very brittle slate-pencil, which shattered if dropped ... and then you copped it! All this was in preparation for doing joined-up writing (known to clever-dicks as the cursive style).

A quick and easy way to clean-off one's slate was to spit on it and then rub it dry with one's sleeve or the nose-rag fastened to one's clothing with a safety-pin.

POLITICS

Unlike Britain, Italy did not have a Conservative or Liberal Party to make their laws. They were ruled by Socialists. A certain journalist broke with that group and formed a party of his own, the Fasci di Combattimento - the Fascists. The man's name was Mussolini.

THE MOVIES

Carnforth folk really enjoyed going to 'The Pictures' in the Station Hotel's Victoria Hall, and were very interested to learn about the film stars whose names were becoming household words. In April, they read that Mary Pickford (The World's Sweetheart), Douglas Fairbanks, Charlie Chaplin and a director named D W Griffiths had teamed up to form their own film distributing company: United Artists. Griffiths was shooting 'Broken Blossoms' with Lilian Gish and, having finished 'Shoulder Arms', Chaplin was at work making 'The Kid' with Jackie Cooper. Those films would be eagerly expected in our town. Lantern slide shows were now considered very 'old hat'!

NEWSPAPERS

After being avidly read, our daily newspapers were not discarded, because households had many uses for them, e.g.:

- Crunched-up into balls, they were used to light the fire, clean the windows or were put inside wet footwear.

- Folded flat they were used as insulation under oil-cloth and lino, placed between wire bed-springs and flock mattresses, or used as absorbent mats when placed around tin baths in front of living-room fires on Friday evenings.

- Cut into neat squares and threaded on to string, which hung from the doors inside earth closets.

- At Spring-cleaning time, they were used to line all drawers and cupboards.

Thrifty Carnforth folk got good value for those newspapers which cost one penny - £1 would cover the cost for 40 weeks.

PROPERTY MATTERS

Because most people rented their homes, 'For Sale' notices were not often seen in our town. Riggs the Builders owned Hill Street and were my parents' landlords. Money was always kept ready on the corner of the mantelpiece for the visit of the rent-collector each week.

Families who were careless about their finances sometimes got deeply into arrears with their rent and had to do a 'moonlight flit', disappearing from the area with all their earthly belongings in a wheel-barrow.

When there were no 'To Let' notices in any house windows, many newly-married couples in Carnforth preferred to go into lodgings rather than remain in their parents' homes. Some householders in New Street, Edward Street, Booker Terrace, Haws Hill etc. were glad to make extra money by subletting.

It was a sad occasion when the last member of a family died. All the contents of the home were put on display on the pavement outside the front door: furniture, items of clothing and foot-wear, personal possessions, pots, pans, cutlery, pictures, photograph albums etc. A very heart-rending sight! A crowd assembled when an auctioneer arrived to sell off the goods and bidding was brisk because the buyers could not afford purchases from shops.

The Barnhams had been brought up to believe that renting a house was an expensive way to nowhere. My parents achieved one of their ambitions when, on February 11th, they purchased 31 Haws Hill for £265 10s through Fawcett and Unsworth (Victoria Buildings, Telephone 3). Signatures were written over a 1d stamp and, for the transaction, the solicitors charged £5 5s.

AMBITIONS

On hearing the news in June that Captain Alock and his navigator, Little Brown, had made the first non-stop flight across the Atlantic Ocean at the incredible speed of 120 mph, some Carnforth lads decided to become airmen when they grew up.

[Sadly, some of them did in World War II.]

None of our girls, however, was inspired to become a politician when it was learnt that Lady Nancy Aster was the first woman to take a seat in Parliament. She dressed very plainly so as not to put off any humble women who might wish to follow in her footsteps. Parliamentary authorities said they had made certain arrangements for any future lady members.

APPAREL

Clothes-conscious people liked to wear garments made specially for themselves. Men could go to a tailor's shop in our town or to the Co-operative Drapery Department in Market Street, where they would be measured-up for a suit - trousers, jacket and waistcoat - chosen from a range of materials and styles.

The Co-op also made ladies' suits, but some people preferred to have their outfits made privately. My father's younger sister, Dora, had served her apprenticeship as a tailoress and dressmaker, and carried out her work at the family home: 38 Grosvenor Place.

She had a selection of Weldon's Fashion books from which her clients made their choice of dresses, suits, underwear, etc. The World of Fashion had decided that dresses would be worn shorter, but Carnforth ladies were not eager to wear daring styles.

For my birthday, I was given a box of paints. It was not necessary to waste money on a colouring book because Auntie Dora gave me her obsolete fashion books.

I enjoyed painting each lady from head to foot in one of the beautiful colours, which had lovely-sounding names: rose-madder, sienna, ultramarine, cobalt blue, emerald green etc.

The women's final at Wimbledon was won by Suzanne Langlen, a daring foreign female, who wore an unusually short dress, loose and sleeveless, which exposed to public view not only her ankles but also her knees. A bandeau across her forehead completed the outrageous sports fashion worn by that startling French woman.

HIGH CHURCH

The original table (1873) of the Parish Church was given posts and gilded angels and became known as The Lady Altar. This caused much controversy among the congregation. Some people wanted the church to stay low, but others agreed with the Reverend Mercer and his high church ideals.

I was very puzzled when I heard my mother complaining that our place of worship was getting too high, so the next time I was taken along Lancaster Road I took a long look at the spire. It was higher than the nearby houses, but in no way as high as the Iron Works chimney. In fact, to me, it appeared to be its usual height, which was right for a church, so why were the grown-ups grumbling about it being too high?

PEACE CELEBRATIONS

On Sunday July 6th, all Carnforth's places of worship joined in the National Day of Thanksgiving for Peace. Special leaflets for the service were used throughout the land.

Carnforth's own Peace Celebrations were held on Saturday July 19th. Crowds assembled on the Market Ground in the morning for a service of thanksgiving. Headmaster R T Barnard read a psalm and the Reverend Mercer gave an address. Our excellent Brass Band led the hymn-singing.

In the afternoon, a Field Day, with sporting events and a fancy-dress parade, was held in Sandford's field up North Road. Dressed as a Red Cross Nurse with a fierce expression, I was photographed holding the handle of my dolls' pram.

BASKETS AND BOXES

It seemed that the majority of Carnforth men worked on the railway because, whatever time of day or night folk went out, they were sure to see some railwaymen, with their baskets or boxes, heading for one of the sheds: the L.N.W.R. Shed, visible from the front windows of Grosvenor Place, the Midland Shed, down Scotland Road, or the Furness Shed, situated to the north-west of the station in the direction of the River Keer.

Carnforth station forecourt. The gateway in the fence (left) leads to the Railwaymen's Institute Building - telegraph poles on the right.

Wicker-baskets had lids that were fastened by means of a metal rod. They contained parcels of sandwiches and cakes, and a flat-sided whiskey bottle full of railwaymen's favourite beverage: cold tea without milk. Tin boxes were larger and their domed lids, which were partitioned off, contained the foot-plate men's rule-books and timetables. The metal boxes were roomy enough to hold several parcels of food because their owners were going to book-off on a double trip, which necessitated an over-night stay at private lodgings or barracks in Carlisle, Crewe, Warrington, Liverpool etc. The crew of one train even stayed at London one night and, from that time on, the driver had a pronounced Cockney accent!

Packing boxes was an important job for railwaymen's wives, and trying to find tasty surprises was difficult. Using a little ingenuity, some foot-plate men enjoyed an unusual fry-up. After being used to toss coal into the fire-box, the long-handled shovel was given a quick wipe with a cleaning-cloth, which every railwayman carried in a pocket of his kytle. A delicious fry-up of bacon, sausage and eggs could then be quickly cooked as the shovel was held in the glowing fire-box.

POINTS TO PONDER

The Government launched an inquiry into London's traffic problems. Carnforth had no such difficulties. Our street-traders' horses were extremely well-behaved, and the few motorcars, which used our roads, were strictly disciplined by the white armlets of a helmeted policeman on point-duty at the busy crossroads, where Market Street intercepts the A6 road at Bank Corner.

Working-class families in our town lived on the bread-winner's earnings of around £75 to £125 per annum. They were thrifty and worked hard to live within their means. To them, the figures which showed that Britain had a national debt of

Busy A6 road looking up towards Fern Bank and Hewthwaite Terrace. House and office of Gasworks manager (left) facing entrance to gravel hole (soon to be a supermarket)

£473,645,000 was absolutely mind-boggling! And we had won the war! "However much is Germany's national debt?" people wondered.

The Cenotaph war memorial was unveiled in London's Whitehall. This information turned Carnforth people's thoughts to the need of a local monument for men of our district, who had died on foreign fields and had no graves here which sorrowing families could tend.

At Greenland's Garage on Scotland Road, petrol now cost 3s 6d per gallon. What expense! A whole guinea to buy 6 gallons. Carnforth folk were glad they could travel cheaply by train and didn't need to worry about the upkeep of a car!

Newspapers reported that a meeting of the German Workers' Party had been addressed by a man called Adolf Hitler. People in our town were uninterested in that information! Who was Adolf Hitler anyway?

German sailors, left aboard 70 captured ships interned at Scapa Flow, raised their double-eagle flags, opened the sea-cocks and scuttled themselves. Good riddance to them!

REMEMBRANCE DAY

On November 11th, the Signing of the Armistice had its first anniversary. Railway engines in the yards blew their whistles at 11am and everybody stopped what they were doing to observe 2 minutes' silence in which to remember the victims of the war, and to give thanks to God for peace.

CHRISTMAS

All over our town, reunited, large family groups squeezed into small sitting-rooms, decorated with lots of holly, to spend a happy Christmas together.

'Our Arthur' didn't need inviting twice to sing his

own theme-song, "Sweet and Low", accompanied by Granddad on his 'squeeze-box' and Uncle Billy on the piano, whilst the rest of the gathering, not musically gifted, did their bit on comb-and-paper, the spoons or bones.

No jungle beasts had, as yet, pounced into Carnforth parlours, but musical tigers were on the loose. The Original Dixieland Jazz Band from America was causing violent enthusiasm when performing on a tour of England. Its leader had composed a tune called 'Tiger Rag', which was bringing audiences to their feet, shouting and clapping in a most unBritish manner!

Tunes sung around Carnforth pianos still tended to be sweet and low.

1920

In January, the Government planned to build 100,000 new houses. Little construction work had been done during the war years, 1914-1918, and all over Britain accommodation was desperately needed for men of the Forces, who were still returning from far-flung battlefields and prisoner-of-war camps.

Over-crowding had now become a serious problem in Carnforth. It was eased a little when, as a start to the proposed new estate, 8 council houses were completed and named Prince Avenue. The chosen tenants felt very proud and privileged.

A TERRIBLE ACCIDENT

A narrow-gauge railway system ran from the Iron Works, for the disposal of hot slag, to the tip on the shore, and also for the transportation of limestone from Scout Quarry, which is situated alongside Silverdale Road. The line branched off to the 2 destinations a short distance behind the pair of semi-detached houses which stand alone, and are name Keer Villas.

Leaving the Iron Works, the little railway crossed a bridge over the Carnforth - Warton Road and ran alongside the Furness Railway Line as far as Keer Villas, where it ran under a small bridge adjacent to the large one used by the Furness Line trains. Small steam engines either pushed or pulled trains of deep sloping-sided trucks along the roughly Y-shaped narrow-gauge system.

One day, an engine, pushing trucks full of fiery slag, blew its whistle as it went under the bridge and approached the junction. At the same instant, another engine, pulling trucks loaded with limestone, sounded its warning. The two trains neither saw nor heard each other and crashed head on. The red hot contents of the trucks were tipped on to their engine at the back and, in the pile-up of trucks and engines, 2 men sadly lost their lives: Mr W J Towers of Carnforth and Mr Daniel Townson of Millhead.

Mr Tower's funeral service was conducted partly at his home and partly at the Congregational Church. The hearse containing his coffin then set off slowly for Warton Churchyard, preceded by 80 workmen and officials of the Iron Works: Mr Linnell, the manager, and Mr Fitton, the engineer.

At Millhead, another 80 workers joined the cortège and, on foot, preceded the coffin of Mr Townson. This was a sad day indeed for the employees of the Iron Works!

[I wish to thank the family of the late Mr Stan Townson of 9 Mary Street, Millhead for this information. He was 4 years old when his father, Daniel, was tragically killed.

The large Towers family once lived at 4 Preston Street: Fred (Bliss), Andy, Arthur, Maggie, Polly, Fanny, Lizzie, Jane, Dinah and Alice, all siblings of 19 year-old Billy, who was killed.

Maggie Towers married Arthur Barnham and their son, my cousin Frank of 25 King Street, also remembers the terrible accident, which saddened the family when he was aged 4.]

THE GOOD SAMARITANS OF MILLHEAD

[It is to Mrs Mary Campbell (née Benson) that I must next give thanks. Born in 1905, she has a remarkable memory of past events in Carnforth, and loves to reminisce. She could rattle skeletons in many local cupboards, but we'll leave sleeping bones to lie!

I feel that that story she told me about the Iron Works accident deserves to be recorded because of the way it reflects the parable of the Good Samaritans. In the Bible story, oil was used to soothe the wounds of the man who fell among thieves, and he was taken to an inn to be cared for until he recuperated. All expenses were willingly paid for by the Samaritan.

Mary's tale tells of the strong bond of neighbourliness which bound together the people of Millhead, whose families had mostly come from the Dudley area to work at the Iron Works, which had been established here in 1864.]

A third victim of the tragic accident, which happened near Keer Villas, suffered horrific burns all over his body. He was taken, not to hospital, *[as would happen today]* but to his home in a Millhead

Terrace, where presumably Dr Jackson visited him. Long strips of cloth soaked in Carron oil and lime-water were wrapped round his body, and needed frequent attention. It can be imagined how grievous was his agony to his loving wife and children. The unpleasant smell of the oil pervaded the little '2-up-2-down' house, but that did not deter caring visitors, who were anxious to offer any help they could give.

The healing process was extremely slow and went on for many, many weeks. All medication and visits from the doctor had to be paid for so, with no bread-winner's earnings coming into the home, the family soon fell on hard times. Friends and relatives took gifts of food and fuel, but the community realised that more help had to be forth-coming. A kind lady volunteered to go round all the houses in Millhead, knocking on doors every week with a collection-box. Every family willingly contributed a few coppers on a regular basis.

There was much rejoicing in the community when, at long last, the husband was well enough to resume work, full of gratitude for the help that had been given to him and his family during their time of need.

Well done, people of Millhead! May your example of how to be true neighbours live on forever!

FUND RAISING EVENTS

The Parish Church, built in 1873, was in need of a

new organ, which would cost the huge sum of £2,000. Many popular fund-raisers of the day had to be organised: Bazaars, Confersaziones, Fancy-dress events, Sales-of-work, Field days, Balls, Whist Drives etc.

In April, the Sunday School teachers arranged for a Children's Ball in the big Co-operative Hall over the 5 shops in New Street. 68 children took part in the Grand March-Round, which opened the event. Mrs Dockray (of the Corn Merchant's family) and the Reverend Mercer were the judges.

It was necessary to hold this part of the programme early on, before any boisterous behaviour wrecked the crêpe paper costumes painstakingly made by fond mothers. Many of the entries were reminiscent of The Great War, e.g.

"Wounded Soldier" (Delhi Murray),
"Rationed" (Seppie Howie),
"War Loan" (Olive Rainbird),
"Red Cross Nurse" (Annie Dawson),
"Soldier's Friend" (Mary Miller) *[How was she dressed-up to represent one of those, I wonder?]*,
"Black-Smith" (Jim Kew),
"House to Let" (Winne Howie),
"Farmer's Boy" (Nellie Williams),
"Grace Darling" (Mary Williams),
"Bubbles" *[a soap advert]*, (Jennie Bagguley),
"Carnforth Knut" (Alan Mason) *[a puzzling costume!]*.

In July, a Field Day was another event to raise money for the Organ Fund.

At 1.30pm, a large crowd assembled on the Market Ground and was led in procession by the Brass Band to Sandford's field up North Road. There, sporting events, races and a Fancy Dress Parade were held. *[It never rained on outdoor events in those days!]*

Sports Field, North Road, July 1920 in aid of the church organ fund. My costume, 'the Allies', won 2nd prize in the Fancy Dress parade.

CARS

Motor vehicles were becoming popular and the Carnforth Motor Company was doing so well that it had its premises on Scotland Road extended. It had started out originally as the Carnforth Cycle Company in an old building adjacent to the

Carnforth Inn.

At the beginning of the year, London police were using cars instead of horses and, in July, it was forecast that by 1921, there would be at least 750,000 motor vehicles on the roads of the United Kingdom, but it was hoped that an alternative to petrol would be found.

Policeman on point duty at the busy crossroads. Hartley's shop on the corner on the right opposite the Bank.

A police report revealed the not very surprising information that the growing number of cars was increasing the number of road deaths! The Ministry of Transport was prepared to bring in an annual tax of £1 per horse-power on privately owned cars.

Two compulsory signals were about to be introduced for all drivers. To signal a turn or slowing down, the driver would have to project his arm horizontally from the right-hand side of the vehicle. The raised arm from the same side would indicate stop.

BILLY SEED

Many tales circulated Carnforth about a mysterious character named Billy Seed who, it appeared, was a few wagons short of a train. During the winter, he was kept very busy down his cellar constructing a fine big cart. By midsummer it was all ready for the road. You're right! He couldn't get it out!

Once he was asked to take 2 wheel-barrows to a farmer in Over Kellet. He whistled gaily as he pushed barrow number one up the long, narrow road. On reaching his destination he looked very puzzled when the farmer said, "Ey man, thou should 'ev put one barra on t' top o' t'uther an' wheeled 'em up together."

"O aye, I nivver thowt about that!" said Billy as realisation dawned on him. He turned round and with a broad smile set off back to Carnforth, trundling barrow number one back again.

It is not known if Billy was a live man or just a fictional character, but he was blamed for many strange happenings and caused lots of laughter.

SCHOOLING

My stay in the Baby Class must have been brief because, during the next 12 months, I was also in the Second Class where Miss Lupton was the teacher <u>and</u> in Miss Jackson's First Class. Perhaps

Miss Jackson and Miss Timperly with First Class at C of E School. Note desks for four pupils and sliding glass partitions.
<u>Front row (left to right)</u>: Connie Walkden, Mary Budd, Gwen Owen.
<u>Middle row</u>: Olive Baines, Annie Boak, Bessie Lowther.
<u>Back row</u>: One girl is Eunice Hoggarth and 3rd along is Agnes Rainford.

they were eager to be rid of my wriggly, restless presence!

Both classrooms had long wooden desks, designed for four children, which had form-like seats attached by means of an iron framework. This arrangement kept two unfortunate children imprisoned in their places by a child at each end. The frequent request, "Please may I leave the room?" caused a lot of manoeuvring which greatly annoyed the teacher.

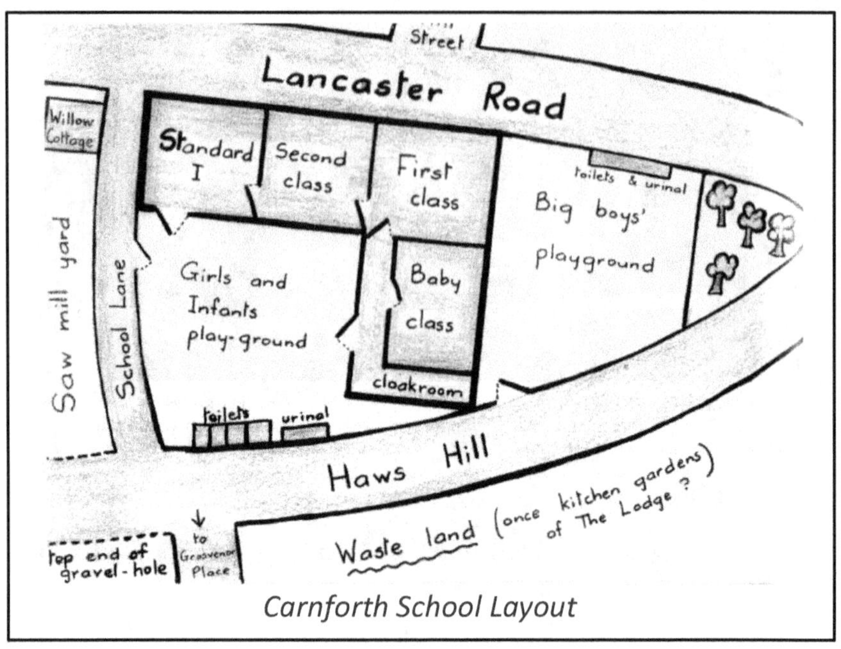

Carnforth School Layout

By each place, a square, divided into 100 small 1-inch squares, was carved into the wooden desk-top. With the aid of cowrie shells (used by West African tribes as coins for barter) we learnt to count and to understand the arithmetical rules of addition, subtraction, multiplication and division.

The 2, 3, 4 and 5 times tables were chanted daily. They all mentioned strange objects, which puzzled our young minds - toozers, freezers, forzers etc. - but such things were of no consequence. As long as we said the numbers correctly, teacher was pleased with us, and we were proud to remember that 3 toozer 6, 6 freezer 18, 2 forzer 8 etc. etc.

We learnt to chant the alphabet: ay, bee, see, dee, ee, ef, gee, aitch, eye, jay etc. Unfortunately we were only taught the names of the letters and did not understand that each produces a sound. We had to repeat after teacher: "See ay tee spells cat" "Bee you dee spells bud" "Dee oh gee spells dog" Memories are not perfect and a child could say, "Pea eye gee spells cow", without knowing why he was wrong.

Miss Timperley and Miss Lupton with Second Class in the grounds of Carnforth Lodge.
<u>Front row (left to right)</u>: (1) Florence Greenwood, (2) Roland Halstead, (4) William Howie, (5) Robert Jackson, (6) Fred Mawson, (7) Walter Rainford, other unknown.
<u>Back row</u>: (3) Marjorie Emmet, (5) Edith Burton, (8) Marian Pennington, (10) Maggie Dugdale.

In the Second and First classes, there was gradual progression from the use of slates to pencil-and-paper work - the paper was squared for figure-work or lined for writing. Letters were not shaped as in the print used in newspapers and books; pot-hooks were used to produce joined-up writing and the letters b, f, g, h, j, k, l and z were formed with loops. A word, when written, did not look the same as when in print. Understandably, learning was very difficult indeed!

On Friday afternoons, big boys collected all inkwells in a bucket for washing out. The headmaster filled them from a big ink bottle on Monday mornings. We hated pens with chewed ends and cross-legged nibs.

PIGGY PETS

Many thrifty Carnforth families kept a pig, which would eat up their scraps and, in return, would eventually provide them with lots of nourishing meals, e.g. pork chops, bacon rashers, trotters etc. Noses indicated the presence of piggeries in the Haws Hill gravel-hole, at the top of Highfield Terrace and, of course, behind Hall Street (formerly Bessemer Terrace), the famous Pig and Parlour row of houses.

Butcher Billy Williams, who had a shop in Market Street and a slaughter-house down Scotland Road, went on his rounds when requested. The members of pig-rearing families closed their doors and windows and covered their ears, in an attempt to shut out the agonised squeals of much-loved pets such as Grunter and Porky, which had to be sacrificed in the furtherance of thrift.

[Mr Jim Taylor, who now lives at Pinner in Middlesex, wrote to tell me that, when his family lived in Hall Street many years ago, he and his sister Zillah loved to play on a swing suspended from hooks in the framework of their back door.

On occasions the swing was removed and the carcass of a pig was hung in its place. Blood which dripped into a utensil placed below was later made into delicious black-puddings]

CONCERNING SHOPS

Half-way down New Street (on the Co-op side) was Garnett's Toffee Shop, which was mostly patronised by adults. My mother loved Thornton's Caramels, Granddad Barnham's favourites were Spanish Buttons, Uncle Arthur had extra-strong mints in all his pockets and my father liked tubes of Life-buoys *[forerunners of Polo mints?]*

When Mr Garnett retired and went to live in Bournemouth, he proudly named his beach-hut "Carnforth."

A rotund gentleman named Harry Gill owned a green-grocer's shop in Victoria Buildings at he bottom of New Street, facing the side of the Station Hotel. Because of his jovial manner and bright beaming face, his fruit and vegetables tasted better than those sold in other shops.

A VISIT TO THE SURGERY

Carnforth people had the choice of 2 doctors: Dr Moss, whose surgery was in his home 72 Lancaster Road (next door to the Bramall family who owned an adjoining Shoe Shop), and Dr Jackson, whose family lived at "Robin Hill" in Market Street. Both the Wilkinsons and Barnhams were patients of the latter. Belle Wilkinson, my father's elder sister, was employed as cook for the doctor's family and was also the nurse for Chitty and Bubbles, his grand-daughters.

Patients entered Robin Hill by a side door. Usually they had to sit for a long time waiting for their turn to see the doctor, but they didn't notice the hardness of the forms around the room because their attention was drawn to glass-fronted cases of stuffed birds and small animals, artistically featured in their natural surroundings, e.g. a snarling fox with a pathetic blood-stained rabbit imprisoned under its foot - not a re-assuring sight for a small child waiting to have its adenoids and tonsils removed! My favourite was a wee 4-legged duckling.

As patients went down the short passage leading to

the consulting room, they could glance into the dispensary on the left, with shelves full of large jars and bottles labelled with strange, long names. They knew what was in the big porcelain container with the word "leeches" printed on it. Ugh!

The white-coated dispenser was usually at work in the room, mixing potions and pouring them into flat-sided medicine bottles, which had graduation marks down one side. Patients had the idea that the only medicine likely to be effective must have a deep colour and a vile taste - the nastier, the more efficacious. Poisonous lotions for external use were always in dark blue ridged bottles, which could be identified in the dark.

All bottles, when firmly corked, were wrapped in white paper and sealed with red sealing-wax, and the dispenser counted out pills, usually pink or white, into tiny round boxes.

The doctor employed a debt-collector to go from door to door accepting a few coppers each week from patients who could not afford to pay their bills.

CURRENT EVENTS TO DISCUSS

- The first 100 women were admitted to Oxford University to study for full degrees. MPs passed the Home Rule Bill for Ireland, which had wanted to break with Britain for many years. The Unionist leader forecast that the Bill would lead to disaster. "Would it?" people wondered.

- Consider this! Fatty Arbuckle, the famous Hollywood comedian whose antics on the screen had amused the picture-goers at the Victoria Hall in the Station Hotel, was charged with the rape and murder of an actress!

- King George V approved of the idea of bringing the body of an Unknown Warrior from a grave on a foreign battlefield, and burying him with full military honours in Westminster Abbey on Armistice Day, November 11th. *[This again turned thoughts to the idea of having a war memorial here in Carnforth.]*

- Four powerful empires had been destroyed in the war - the German, Austrian, Russian and Turkish - and, since 1918, there had been many discussions about the re-drawing of the map of Europe. Now two new countries were created: Czechoslovakia and Yugoslavia - strange names for places which the children of Carnforth were sure they would never visit.

BAN BOOZE?

At the beginning of the year, Prohibition had been introduced in America, and the manufacture and sale of alcohol had been forbidden. The law was difficult to enforce however, and gang-warfare and boot-legging were causing a great deal of crime.

On moral grounds, some people wanted Prohibition to be made law in Scotland and, towards the end of the year, a fierce campaign was waged between the 'Wets' (the whisky-distillers and licensees) and the 'Dries' (the strong Non-Conformist Church). Voters in the dispute received a deluge of leaflets from both sides, 'The Wets' showering their literature from aircraft, bearing on their wings the slogan, 'Vote No Change'. They eventually won the campaign.

In Carnforth there were fierce arguments on the topic between the Salvation Army, the Methodist Chapel and the organisers of the Band of Hope, all on one side, versus the men who loved to booze at their local pubs on the opposite side.

BUSY MACHINES

Being an only child can be a lonely state of life, especially at night-time. When my mother had put me to bed and gone downstairs with the candle, a sense of desolation could overcome me as I listed to the faint, solemn sound of classical music played by our next-door neighbour, Mrs Fred Taylor, who was an accomplished pianist.

My little Kelly-lamp shone like a star, but did not illuminate the corners of the room where scary boggarts might be lurking in the darkness, and creepy-crawlies with long hairy legs might come down the chimney of the little fireplace against which my big double-bed pressed.

Like all thrifty Carnforth women, my mother used her peaceful evenings for sewing. She was an expert machinist and the zooming sound of her Jones Treadle Machine reassured me of her presence and I was eventually soothed to sleep.

New sheets were made by hemming large pieces of unbleached cotton material. Old sheets were patched or turned sides to middle, but when patches needed patching, it was decided that the sheets had reached the end of their lives and they were then recycled into bolster-cases, pillow-cases, ironing-clothes, tea-towels, dusters, nappies, sanitary towels or just left as pieces of material suitable for bread poultices, roly-poly dumplings etc.

Dresses, blouses, skirts, petticoats, nighties, bodices, camisoles and singlets were skilfully made from cheap remnants or the good parts of discarded garments. At some houses, father's worn-out trousers were cut down to make little Willie a grand pair of pants, and grandma's old nightie could be recycled to make a petticoat for young Mary. 'Waste not, want not', was a proverb frequently quoted!

Silverdale Agricultural Society held a locally-famous Exhibition each summer, and my mother was keen to enter her work in the Arts and Crafts Section For Ladies. She specialised in machining men's shirts, and there was rivalry for First Prize between her and Mrs Maggie Carruthers, who lived on Hewthwaite Terrace. My mother was also a frequent winner in the classes for invisible patching on both plain and patterned material.

The sewing-machines in Carnforth homes saved many £s for thrifty families.

CROWDED BEDROOMS

Lonely bedrooms did not worry many Carnforth children. Quite the opposite! One of the two bedrooms in a Ramsden Street house was long and narrow, and a certain large family of 11 children had to have two double beds, placed end to end so that the boys had to climb over to reach the other.

There was space for only one other item of furniture: a chair - no wash-hand-stand, no dressing-table, no wardrobe. This meant that there were no drawers for clothes, which had to be either in wear, in the wash or airing, layer upon layer, on a clothes-rack suspended from the ceiling near the living-room fireplace. Racks were raised or lowered by means of a rope and pulley arrangement.

MOTORISED TRANSPORT

Great excitement among the children! Strange vehicles caused much interest on our main road - large, red and not pulled by horses! They were Lambsfield's Omnibuses on their route between Lancaster and Warton.

Local bus outside the Kinema in Market Street, 1925. Centre is Dr Jackson's home and surgery on Robin Hill.

They were a wonderful novelty but, as most Carnforthians belonged to railway families, they remained faithful to the train by heading for our very busy railway station when they wanted to go shopping to Lancaster.

SILENT FILMS

During Autumn, people on their way to the railway station or the Post Office were intrigued to see a large building under construction on the piece of spare land, which faced The Station Hotel at the bottom of Market Street. "Whatever was it going to be?" folk wondered. Rumours about a picture-house caused great excitement.

It did indeed become a magnificent picture-house, with an impressive, pillared façade reminiscent of a Greek or Roman temple. It was said that it was probably the most up-to-date edifice in the area.

It cost £8,000 and local people eagerly bought shares in the company concerned. The auditorium and balcony would seat 500 on tip-up, plush-upholstered seats - what luxury after the hard wooden forms at the Victoria Hall!

A 14HP gas engine and dynamo lit up the building with electricity.

"The Kinema", (telephone 11), Managing Director, William Weeks, was opened on December 18th. It promised rock-steady projection for high-class and popular pictures, which could be seen for reasonable prices: 6d and 9d 'downstairs' and 1s 3d and 1s 10d 'upstairs' in the balcony.

A stupendous programme was advertised for Christmas Day!

A typical programme consisted of:

- The Big Picture: a romantic drama, perhaps featuring Mary Pickford and Douglas Fairbanks.

- A Comedy Film: Maybe Charlie Chaplin and Jackie Coogan.

- A Serial: hair-raising episode of a film with Pearl White or Nazimova tied to a railway line and left there till the next episode the following week.

- The Pathé News.

CHRISTMAS ONCE MORE

As the year drew towards its close and plans for Christmas Day were discussed, there was, for the first time in our town's history, an attractive alternative to the traditional, family Parlour Party with renderings of mournful melodies of old-timers, such as "I dreamt I dwelt in Marble Halls", spiced-up with the year's favourite songs, "Margie" and "Avalon."

Keen movie-goers formed queues outside the Kinema, but not everyone in Carnforth approved of this form of entertainment. Later that week, angry letters appeared in the Lancaster Guardian from religious people, mainly Salvationists and Wesleyans, who called the new picture-house a 'Den of Iniquity'. They wrote that the money spent on it should have been used instead for the building of houses, which were greatly needed. They declared that moving-pictures deprived people of their brain power!

1921

When the ten-yearly census was taken, it was learnt that Carnforth had 3,247 inhabitants, an increase of only 105 since the last count in 1911.

Our population had grown very rapidly in the second half of the 19th century, from 294 in 1851 to 3,040 in 1901. Few houses had been built since then and expansion was nearly at a standstill.

DEPRESSION

Carnforth's economic problems were a reflection of those facing the country. Great Britain was in recession and unemployment figures topped 2 million during the year, the numbers being swollen by thousands of ex-servicemen out of work or on short time.

Since the Armistice, there had been an explosion in the price of goods, and the Government had had to raise dole money from 15 to 18 shillings per week for men, and from 12s to 15s for women.

Carnforth felt the depression deeply and out-of-work ex-servicemen were glad to spend some of their unwanted spare-time at The British Legion Club (or Comrades as it was also known) - a wooden hut down Scotland Road. Over-worked housewives were not pleased about that!

GENTLEMEN OF THE ROAD

Wearing several layers of ragged overcoats tied

around the waist with a length of string, tramps were frequently to be seen trekking along our north - south highway.

They were wise enough to knock only at the back doors in Hill Street. My mother would willingly give them a pint-pot of sweet tea and a 'doorstep' cheese sandwich, providing they sat out in the back street, well away from our house.

If ever she spared them a copper, she stipulated that it must not be wasted on booze, but should go towards the cost of a night's rest at the 3-storey Lodging House, with an oddly-shaped roof, in Millhead.

Scruffy Joe, who had long, straggly whitish hair and a grey beard, was king of the tramps.

LADIES LIKEWISE

Thin, sad-faced street-singers, wrapped in ragged black shawls, used to trail slowly down our front street, wailing their miserable songs. Kindly neighbours would take the women a penny or a ha'penny.

One afternoon, when my mother was busy in the back-kitchen, I rushed in from school, ashen-faced. "There's a nasty old witch asleep on our sofa!" I gasped. Yes, we'd had an unexpected caller. A weary street-singer had seen our open front door as an invitation to pop in and have a comfy nap.

ORGAN FUND ... AGAIN

The congregation of the Parish Church was still working hard to raise money for a new organ. Once again a Children's Fancy Dress Ball was organised and, by this time, the war years were nearly overlooked, except by Mollie Lowther as "Peace" and May Scriven as "Rule Britannia".

Topical costumes were "Crossing Sweeper" (Eric Lowther), "Organ Grinder" (Bessie Bagguley) and "Cocoa Nibs" - an advert of the day by Rowntree's (Marion Wilkinson (Me!) and my cousin, Billy Barnham.)

THE AUCTION MART

Carnforth was all abustle on Mondays as farmers from a wide surrounding area arrived here by pony-and-trap for the Auction Mart, which was held behind the Queen's Hotel in Market Street.

The animals to be sold were driven here along the roads by farm-workers, and put into iron pens to await the arrival of the auctioneer.

On occasions, some of the cattle being driven 'on the hoof' became obstreperous and raced off down one of Carnforth's side-streets. One day, quite uninvited, a cow called in on a startled young wife at her home in Edward Street. It was not given a warm welcome.

Another time an angry bull - yes! It was a bull, it had horns to prove the point - charged down Hill

Street and rushed through the open door of Number 28. There, it became firmly wedged by its horns in the narrow passage. Men pushed it at the back and pulled it at the front whilst wives stood by giving orders. Children bounced about in excitement at this unexpected adventure.

The poor animal must have been freed eventually, because it is not remembered that neighbours enjoyed any extra beef that week!

The Queen's Hotel was a very busy place on Auction Mart days. Farming folk enjoyed the substantial English Fare which could be ordered, and chatted about rural matters as they drank foaming glasses of fine ale.

Li'l Teddy Pennington was usually in their midst, and high-spirited farmers kept 'treating' him because they liked to see him the worse for drink. The little fellow was a dwarf about 3 ft tall and, with his longish hair, moustache, walking-stick and bowler hat, he looked like a shortened cross between David Lloyd George and Charlie Chaplin. Living in Lancaster, he was a well-known character in our locality.

He made a livelihood by selling monkey-nuts (in their shells) from his large wicker basket, and was a familiar figure in Lancaster Market. Naughty children taunted him unmercifully and screeched with delight when he waved his walking-stick at them. Mothers thought he was very 'skinny' with his nuts, because he kept his fat thumb in the tin mug he used as a measure.

Arthur Cockerham, the landlord, advertised the Queen's Hotel as, "The best of accommodation with very comfortable rooms."

It was the headquarters for Carnforth Rangers Associated Football Club, Carnforth and District Athletic Club, and Carnforth and District Poultry Association.

Most animals bought at the Auction Mart were driven along the roads to their new homes by farm-labourers, but some were led down to Carnforth Railway Goods Yard (entrance down Warton Road) and kept in pens there whilst waiting for transport by train.

My encounter with a group of cows, once, gave me nightmares for many months. They were being driven along Lancaster Road when one fierce beast charged towards me as I was on my way to buy some sausages at the Co-op butcher's (manager, Mr Bristowe) at the top end of New Street. I dashed into the shop panic-stricken, with a horn of the ferocious creature only a few inches from one leg of my lace-edged knickers.

The bull braked sharply at the shop door-way, faced with a terrible sight. Chopped neatly in half and suspended from large hooks along one wall was a row of his brothers and sisters, dripping blood on to the sawdust-covered floor. Ugh!

SCHOOL MEMORIES

Miss Taylor, a foreign lady with a strange accent, taught Standard I. This was the top class 'downstairs' at the Church of England School and a certain standard of education had to be attained before scholars could be lined up, marched across the play-ground and led upstairs to Standard II in the Big School.

Multiplication tables up to 12 times had to be learnt and the 4 rules (addition, subtraction, multiplication and division) of 'Tens and Units' and 'Shillings and Pence' sums had to be mastered.

'Running-hand' writing had to be done between double lines on pages of blue-backed note-books. All work was done with pen and ink, and frequent exercises were Dictation, which demonstrated one's inability to spell, and Compositions, the titles of which ensured that nosy teachers could acquire an intimate knowledge of their pupils' family lives.

Dual desks, with tops and seats which could be raised, were arranged in neat rows - girls on the right, boys on the left.

THE CLASS OF 1921

There was a pleasant break in lesson routine on June 10th (my 6th birthday) when a visiting photographer arrived to take a class picture in the playground. What a palaver it was to get the children arranged neatly in 3 rows: standing at the

The Class of 1921, CofE School. June 10th (my birthday).
Back row (left to right): Chris Peddar, unknown, Olive Clement, Kathy Owen, Freda Haycock, Janet Askew, Mary Wilkinson, Maggie Jones, Mavis Stockton, Edith Burton, Flossie Mawson.
Middle row: Florence Greenwood, John Russell, Laura Moorby, Lizzie Ashworth, Marion Wilkinson, Gladys Robertson, Edna Astley, Freda Taylor, Lizzie Shaw, Jim Stephenson, Betty Stephenson, Jack Wilson, Wilfred Ireton.
Front row sitting: Bertie Dumblelton, Bob Jackson, Jimmy Walkden, Freddie Whittam, Roland Halstead, Jack Astley, Freddie Mawson, John Cook, Jim Ormand, Robert Jackson, Normal Cresswell, Tom Wilkinson.

back, seated on forms in the middle and cross-legged on the ground in front. The chap kept disappearing under a black cloth to view the scene through the lens of his camera, which was mounted on a tripod stand. His patience was sorely tried when several highly-strung children, finding all the excitement too much for them, timidly requested, "Please sir, may I leave the playground?"

It was apparent which children came from homes where dads had good jobs, probably on the railway. Some boys looked like young princes in velvet suits with pearl buttons and big white collars, whilst the girls had pretty white broderie anglaise pinafores with epaulettes worn over smart dresses.

The unfortunate children from big families, whose fathers had lost their jobs at the Iron Works, wore patched or ragged clothes and had clogs on their feet.

[Four of the children in the photograph lost their lives in World War II: Jim Stephenson, an army officer; Jim Walkden, a soldier; Bertie Dumbleton, a sailor aboard HMS Penelope when it sank off the shores of Crete; and Jack Astley, an airman who was shot down over Yugoslavia.]

PARTY TIME

One of the highlights of this school year was the Christmas Party, when we children sat at our desks and enjoyed brawn sandwiches, assorted cakes (13, a baker's dozen, for one shilling (5p) sold at Jackson's Café in Market Street) and cups of tea filled from a shiny, brass tea-urn.

The most thrilling event of the jolly afternoon was a Monkey Nut Scramble. We stood in a large circle around the room and Miss Taylor (who by the way came from Ireland) threw a big handful of nuts in their shells into the centre. When she blew her whistle, that was the signal for everyone to dash forward and grab as many nuts as possible. Naturally the big rough boys came off best, whilst gentle little girls remained in the places ... nutless!

PROFITABLE PASTIMES

Railway employees were able to rent land alongside the track, and those whose homes did not have a garden or a nearby allotment were pleased to avail themselves of the privilege. Men used their spare time to rear hens, pigs and goats, tend vegetable and flower gardens and pamper pigeons in lofts.

[Jogging as a form of exercise was unheard of, and quite unnecessary.]

My grandfather Wilkinson had a hen-run perched high on top of the embankment at the southern end of the station and, to reach it, I remember climbing with my father up a steep side of Haws Hill gravel-hole, balancing on a tin basin full of Indian corn (maize) which smelled nice enough to eat, but was as hard and tasteless as pebbles. I loved feeding the hens and was intrigued to learn that they existed in interesting varieties: Plymouth Rocks, Rhode Island Reds, Black Leghorns and White Wyandottes. It puzzled me that birds, fishes and dogs are to be found in wonderfully differing forms, whilst all people are just people, their skin colour differences merely depending upon exposure to the sun!

After I'd fed and watered the hens, I enjoyed chopping-up broken pieces of crockery very finely on a big flat stone. This grit was added to the hens' staple diet of boiled potatoes, mixed with meal from Dockray's warehouse, to ensure that they laid eggs with firm shells and gave the cocks something to crow about.

My father rented an adjacent piece of land to grow vegetables. Whilst he was busy digging, I sat in the tall grass nearby, nibbling delicious peas straight from the pod and watching fussy shunt-engines sorting out clink-clanking wagons and forming them into trains in the busy L.N.W.R. marshalling yard way down below.

Every now-and-again, express trains would shrill their whistles as they whooshed through the station, leaving clouds of smoke and steam in their wake.

CHURCH WAR MEMORIALS

On Sunday July 17th at 2.00pm, a service was held in the Parish Church for the 'Unveiling and Dedication of a Memorial Window', in remembrance of the 50 men who had died in the war. 'The Dead March' in Saul was played on the organ The Last Post and the Reveille were sounded by a bugle, and Colonel E North gave an address and unveiled a Memorial Tablet.

The Brass Band and representatives of the Comrades of the Great War attended a moving service at the Congregational Church, when a 2-Light Stained Glass Window was unveiled in memory of their 13 church members who had fallen in the war. Panel 1 depicted a Red Cross Nurse tending a wounded soldier. Panel 2 portrayed St George, and had the names of the fallen inscribed on it.

CONCERNING CHILDREN

- Being sent on an errand to the Co-op Confectionary Department (the bottom of the Society's 5 shops in New Street) was a very scary experience for little girls, because the shop was managed by a fiery dragoness named Miss Bond. They were glad to escape, uneaten, with a tissue-paper-wrapped loaf in their mothers' wicker shopping baskets. *[In later years, when the department was moved to the top shop, it is vaguely remembered that the dragoness had a pleasant assistant named Annie Mingings].*

- In cold weather, children could always be seen leaning against the wall of a bake-house in Preston Street next to the Salvation Army building. It belonged to Jackson's Café and was lovely and hot. Delicious smells wafted from the window and occasionally lucky children were fed tit-bits.

- Little girls bounced their balls and sang,

"One, two, three Alaira, I saw my Auntie Claira ..." (what auntie was up to varied from street to street!)

- Colbeck's Chemist Shop *[later Fletchers's]*, 30 Market Street, sold thick, hard sticks of LIQUORICE ('Spanish'). Mothers broke up 1 pennyworth with their rolling-pins and children popped the bits into medicine bottles which were filled with water, and then shaken very vigorously. Lacy froth formed at the top of the bottles and this could be sucked-up and enjoyed immediately, but the liquid darkened and become more potent if left to mature in a dark place, probably under the side-board, right at the back. Spanish water was a must in every child's life, but most kiddies were glad when they'd had enough - it wasn't at all nice! Yellow crystals of Khali bought at a toffee-shop made a much better drink, all nice and lemony.

- Children, wearing their best clothes, did not enjoy solemn Sunday walks to church-yards. Week-day walks, however, could be interesting and exciting. They were taken for what they might produce rather than for exercise. Walking-sticks could be used as weapons to ward off fierce beasts, and were useful implements for the collection of hazel-nuts, holly, acorns to give to pigs, and crab-apples for mothers to make into jelly.

Cowslips, Dandelions and Primroses made delicious wines, and Chickweed was fed to canaries. Watercress was found in the stream in Springfield, and Mushrooms abounded in fields rich in 'cow-pats'. To decorate and brighten-up our homes, there was a wealth of wild flowers and Doddering grass.

- The children at Cobbe's School (The Church of England) had lots of giggles and sniggers about a funny little Indian fellow called Gandhi. "He werc all bur except fer a grut, baggy nappy!" He'd some cheek though. He boycotted the visit of our Princes of Wales to India, and organised a civil disobedience campaign.

COAL-IN-THE-HOLE

Thrifty members of the Carnforth Railway Coal Club were not anxious when coal rationing was introduced due to miners being on strike, because they had good stocks in their cellars. When ordered, their loads of coal were delivered from the Goods Yard by horse-and-cart and deposited on their fronts. It was heavy work shovelling a ton of coal down the small circular hole near their door-steps - and "a reet mucky job an' all!" - but members thought that the effort was worthwhile when they considered the money saved. Buying a one hundredweight sack per week worked out much more expensive at 3 shillings each.

POINTS FOR PARENTS TO PONDER

- Legal history was made this year when six women were sworn-in to sit on a Divorce Court Jury. It was feared they'd be shocked by case details - abominable letters and disgusting pictures. The women agreed not to look at such!

- The first Birth Control Clinic, founded by Marie Stopes, was opened in London. There was bitter opposition from the clergy, who feared it would encourage immorality.

- Sunday postal collection and delivery was ended.

- The fiftieth anniversary of the first Bank Holiday lead to packed excursion trains and charabancs heading for the seaside.

- A man named Adolf Hitler was voted President of the National Socialist Workers' Union.

- A second woman took her seat in Parliament.

- At the Kinema, Rudolf Valentino set hearts aflutter when he appeared in "The Sheikh".

- Medical history was made with the use of insulin for sufferers of diabetes.

- Benito Mussolini declared himself 'Il Duce', leader of the National Fascist Party in Italy.

- There was mounting alarm over the latest fashions in women's dresses, which were claimed to be immodest and immoral. Skirts, which had kept rising since the war, now revealed calves of legs. One American state was considering the imprisonment of inappropriately dressed women. Fashionable young women, named flappers, were trying to emulate men - flat chests, straight-up-and-down clothes and short hair. There were worries that loose behaviour would be encouraged when combined with other disturbing modern trends such as drinking, smoking, using make-up and doing the latest wild dances, like The Charleston and The Blackbottom. Would the girls at Morphy's Mill defy their mothers and try out some of the modern fashions? Tongues wagged and fingers waved!

A MERRY CHRISTMAS

Joyous carols rang out from the newly-installed organ on December 24th. A successful climax to the Parish Church Fund had been reached at last. The congregation was proud because it was said that the new organ was the finest two-manual instrument in the north of England.

1922

There was still a great deal of poverty in Britain when the New Year dawned. One and a half million people were on Poor Relief - the highest ever recorded! The Ministry of Health told Islington Council that £3 13s 6d was too much money to give to a family on relief!

Public-spirited people in Carnforth formed a Distress Fund Committee and poor children, whose fathers were out-of-work, took basins and spoons to the C of E and the Council school where they were given hot soup to sustain them. Not forgetting that there were even more poverty-stricken families elsewhere, the ladies of the Distress Committee collected out-grown clothes here, and made them up into parcels for dispatch. My mother received a thank-you letter from a family in Tamworth, who had received one of my coats, in the pocket of which she had put a message of goodwill.

UNKNOWN STREETS

Although there were no houses in them, the side streets behind some of our terraces had names, which were unfamiliar to most inhabitants. George Street led to Preston Street from John Street. John Street connected New Street with Preston Street. Derby Road led from Stanley Street to Oxford Street. Cross Street ran behind Derby Road. Church Street led to the back of Lancaster Road (near the church). Dalton Road, off Highfield Terrace, led to Russell Road. Poole Street, rear of Highfield Terrace and back of Russell Road. Walmsley Street, back of Scotland Road from Market Street. Railway Street, alongside the Motor Company Garage from Market Street (west).

MOBILE SHOPS!

If necessary, people could get all they needed brought to their doors, without having to go 'down the street' to the shops - a boon for old people, the disabled and mothers with babies and toddlers!

1. JOHNNY BLACKBURN

Johnny Blackburn was one of Carnforth's well-known travelling tradesmen, who sold fish, kippers and rabbits from a flat cart pulled by a faithful horse.

His main stand was at the bottom of Market Street in front of The Kinema, but frequently he stopped in a strategic position in some central back-street and rang his famous hand-bell to summon housewives from several streets at the same time (e.g. by taking his stand in Derby Road his bell could be heard at the backs of Lancaster Road, Oxford Street and Stanley Street). Some of Johnny's boxes of fish arrived by rail from Fleetwood, and local farmers kept him well-supplied with rabbits, which he could skin at record speed. A pair of kippers cost about 5d.

2. POSSIES'S

Postlethwaites had a hardware shop on Lancaster Road, and William and his son Bob traded round Carnforth and nearby villages with their horse and cart. They sold buckets, pan-menders, candles, night-lights, black-lead, donkey-stones, flat irons, clothes-lines, pegs, lamp-wicks and chamber-pots (poes, jerries, gozzunders and other less polite euphemisms). Those essential 'night-jars' were not all made of plain white pottery - some had dainty floral patterns with roses, lilies, or perhaps more appropriately sweet-peas!

3. AN INDUCEMENT

A well-known character called "Old Deerfoot" lived in a hut in the Spring Field. He went round our streets with his cart, selling not watercress, as might have been expected, but firewood. It was reported that his horse refused to go up Edward Street unless it was given a carrot by a kindly lady who lived there.

4. HYGIENE

A family, who did odd-job trading using their horse and cart, lived in one of the end of Bank Terrace. The cart was kept on adjacent spare land but the horse was 'stabled' in the passage of their home. Because the animal had not responded to house-training, a bucket was tied under its tail to observe the niceties of hygiene.

Mr. William Postlethwaite ('Possie') with his horse, Lady, and his dog, Beauty. He and his son, Bob, came on their rounds in the 1920s.

5. CARTS FOR HIRE

Battersby's, from whom people could hire a flat cart, had their premises in an old barn alongside Lancaster Road, near the junction with Haws Hill. *[This old building, later used as a Tyre-service Centre, was eventually demolished in the late 1970s.]*

6. RAGS AND BONES!

Children pricked-up their ears, stopped whatever they were doing and started to pester their parents when they heard the raucous street-cry, "Ra-a-a-g a'bone!"

If they could wheedle a bundle of unwanted odds and ends from mum or dad, the Rag-and-Bone man would exchange it for a lovely blown-up balloon.

He made his living by selling the rubbish he collected with his horse and cart: Bones (for glue and manure), Rags, which were unpicked for various manufacturing purposes, such as the production of shoddy cloth, jars, bottles, paper etc. *[In fact he was an environment-friendly expert - a useful early spoke in the Recycling Wheel!]*

7. ALIVE ALIVE HO!

Dressed in a thick, navy-blue jersey and thigh-high waders, a fisherman from across the Bay (Kents Bank or Flookburgh) came to Carnforth by train each week and sold flukes, cockles and mussels from his barrow as he went round our streets.

Like other housewives, my mother put a pan of water on the fireside hob, tipped in some mussels, sprinkled oatmeal over them so that they would open their shells to release sand, and then gave them a quick boiling.

When cooked, they were taken from their shells, and a dangerous bit of weed was pulled out of each mussel. Then followed a quick and hopeful inspection for pearls.

My mother never managed to make herself a link such as was worn by Queen Mary, but at the bottom of a small glass phial, once full of shining silver balls for the decoration of cakes, were a few teeny-weeny, non-gleaming, but much treasured pearls!

8. FORBIDDEN FRUIT

Because the trade of Mr Waghorne of the Peg Leg did not cover the whole of Carnforth, Mr Archie Brown also had a round, and sold fruits and vegetables from his cart. Produce was of non-exotic varieties: boxes of apples, oranges, bananas, pears and grapes, protected by cork chipping in small barrels.

Vegetables varied with the season: potatoes, carrots, onions, cabbages, swedes, cauliflowers, beans and peas. Archie was a very pleasant, persuasive salesman and the lads (never girls!) of the Ramsden Street, Hunter Street district realised that, when he called in at the home of a certain lady, he would be there for quite a while, attempting to persuade her to taste of his wares.

This gave the boys the opportunity to play around the cart, swinging from it and wobbling it about. When apples and oranges bounced out of their boxes and rolled on to the road, they could joyfully be picked up and eaten with no guilty feelings.

A CLEAN SWEEP

Another familiar character to be seen around our town, with his 3-wheeled hand-card and busy brushes, was Joe Naylor, famous for his 2 left feet. He was our Street Sweeper and his equipment was kept in the Council hut on the Market Ground.

We children raced him to pick up the empty

Players' cigarette packets from the gutters. Oh, the thrill of finding one with a fag-card still inside which would complete one of the famous Sets of 50 cards: 'Flags of all Nations', 'Do You Know?', 'Wonders of the World', 'Ships', 'Film Stars' etc. New fag-cards had a really exciting smell!

SALVATION

After pounding the roads all week, those three men, Joe Naylor, Johnny Blackburn and William Postlethwaite could have been forgiven if, on a Sunday morning, they had indulged in a well-earned 'sleep-in'. But no! They arose with the lark, donned their Salvation Army uniforms and headed for the Hall in Preston Street - a simple construction of corrugated-iron originally, but later improvement had converted it into a more permanent brick building.

Joe, Johnny and William were faithful members of the excellent S A Band, which marched proudly along our streets as they played rousing hymn-tunes, stopping at three locations to preach the gospel and declare their faith to one and all every Sunday.

HORSES

Tradesmen's horses were renowned for their patience but, on some occasions, that virtue became exhausted. The driver of a Co-op cart, which paid weekly visits to the surrounding villages, was in the habit of putting a nose-bag over his horse's head whilst he popped into the local pub for some liquid refreshment.

At Silverdale one afternoon, the weary animal had long since munched all its lunch, but still the driver had not emerged to continue his round. Enough was enough! The horse set off on the long walk to the warehouse behind the grocery department shop in New Street, where its arrival caused amazement amongst the staff. Imagine the consternation on the face of the driver when he eventually tottered unsteadily from the pub. There was his horse and cart - gone!

NUMBER ONE AND NUMBER TWO

It seemed that no roundsmen ever succeeded in street-training their horses. Their malodorous streams, flowing along the streets, caused 'snewed-up' noses and disgusted expressions, especially in hot weather!

Their big jobs however were greeted with smiles of welcome. Folk rushed out their front doors with buckets and shovels in a mad race to win the steaming 'coddies' which were such rich manure for back-gardens and allotments. They worked wonders on rhubarb. *[Please don't say you have custard on yours!]*

CONCERNING RELIGION

- The Congregational Church had lovely ideas to encourage children to join 'The League of

Young Worshippers'. On 'Snowdrop Sunday' and 'Hyacinth Sunday', they took to church flowers which they had grown from bulbs, given to them earlier by Mrs Towers, the Minister's wife. Clifton Helliwell, whose mother had a High Class Ladies' Shop in Market Street, played the organ.

[Clifton was a gifted musician who eventually became a piano soloist with the BBC and accompanied many famous singers.]

- Mr Mercer, vicar of the Parish Church, introduced altar candlesticks which, once again, upset those members of the congregation who were against our church 'going high'. *[Vestments were also introduced the following year and caused more trouble.]*

- People of the 'Mission' faith held services and Sunday School meetings in the Iron Works Room on Warton Road.

- Children whose families were not well-off and couldn't afford to take them on holidays or trips became members of as many Sunday Schools as possible. This was in order to qualify them to go on several summer outings. The Parish Church frequently took its Sunday School children by train to Grange, where refreshments were eaten in the Parish Room of a local church.

ROYAL WEDDING

Playing at weddings was always a favourite childhood game, and it became very popular when pictures appeared in all the newspapers of the marriage of Princess Mary, the only daughter of King George V and Queen Mary, to Viscount Lascelles.

Any girl who was lucky enough to be given an old lace curtain could claim to be the bride at a backyard wedding although, on occasions, some Bossie Bessie would demand the role.

Wearing a pair of high-heeled shoes bought at a jumble sale and carrying a beautiful bouquet of dog-daisies and dandelions, the bridge was the envy of all the other little girls, who had to be content to form a bevy of bridesmaids.

A bridegroom, tall, dark and handsome, was conspicuous by his absence. Because boys flatly refused to join in, all the players at 'weddings' were female, and that included the vicar!

[At that time, the idea of a lady vicar was unthinkable.]

THE SLIDING STONE

On the Market Ground was a huge, limestone rock - steep on one face, gently sloping on another. Because of their proximity to it, the children of Carnforth's Lake District considered that the sliding stone belonged to them. They tried to drive away any other kiddies who queued-up for an exciting slide.

Many were the backsides of breeches and knickers worn out on that stone.

[The rock can be clearly seen on photographs of the Unveiling of the War Memorial in 1924. It is said that some years later a huge hole was dug beside the stone which was then pushed into it and buried.]

EGYPTOLOGY

One day in November, Mr Strangeways, (and he certainly had 'em!) the master of Standard 6 at the Church of England School, told his class that Howard Carter, the archaeologist, had made a wonderful discovery at Luxor in Egypt. It was the tomb of Tutankhamen in the Valley of the Kings, and it was packed with the young Pharaoh's priceless treasures which had been buried for over 3,000 years.

The children were very interested. A stuffed king! They chattered about the amazing discovery as they clattered down the iron steps, which led from their upstairs classroom down the outside of the building to the girls' playground below.

LANCASTER STATION

Carnforth young people with a copper or two to spare found that a wait on Lancaster Railway Station could be an exciting experience.

They could enjoy:

- A drink of water from a heavy lead beaker attached by a chain to the 'fountain' in the wall of Platform 1. (Germs included, free of charge!)

- Make a metal strip with their name on it by inserting 1d into a clever machine, and moving a pointer on a clock-like arrangement of letters of the alphabet.

- Obtain 5 Woodbine fags in a paper packet from a machine, when 2d was put into it (and parents weren't looking).

- Get a wrapped bar of Cadbury's chocolate from another machine, in exchange for 1d.

My most exciting memory of the station was how, whilst waiting for the train from Preston to bring us home, I learnt how to ride a miniature bicycle. My parents had just bought me a fairy-cycle for my 7th birthday from Lawson's wonderful toy-shop, in Lancaster's New Street, well-known for the real rocking horse which was its shop-sign.

DOLLS, DOLLS, DOLLS

I was the mother of a family of dolls of various sizes and varieties: celluloid dolls, dolls with sawdust-filled bodies and pot heads and limbs; baby dolls with sleeping eyes - which slipped down into their hollow bodies if not handled gently - girl dolls with jointed arms and legs, a teddy-bear, and a magnificent fairy doll with dress, crown and magic wand of sparkling silver. Actually, the fairy was more an ornament than a toy, and was a sad disappointment when the silver tarnished and its waxen complexion lost its beauty.

My dolls lived a life of luxury. They had a pram and a bed, both with pretty covers, a celluloid toilet-set with jug-and-basin, soap dish, brush and comb etc. and even wash-day equipment, with miniature tub, mangle, clothes-maid and clothes posts with a line.

[Very sexist toys. We small maidens were being trained to do household chores!]

On warm days, my mother spread her oldest pegged rug on the grassy part of our shared backyard, and carried out my dolls and a wooden box, once used for margarine, full of dolls' clothes. Agnes Rainford, Freda Taylor, Ethel Ashton and other good friends would come and play.

William Howie was the only boy who would join in our game. Being the youngest, and only, boy in a large family meant that he was used to female toys. (They had run out of girls' names when their last daughter arrived, so she was called The Seventh: Septima.) William, however, refused to be my dolls' daddy and I was glad about that, because his temper and bad language were not appropriate for the parent of a happy family.

"Put your *** arm in this *** sleeve!" he'd shout at

my best doll, Winnie, named after his very own sister, who was my favourite big girl.

Like an express train emerging from a tunnel, my mother would charge out of our back door and send William home in disgrace until he had washed-out his mouth with soap and water, and was ready to be a good boy again.

When any of my dolls were in need of medical attention, they were taken to Lawson's Dolls' Hospital where joints were repaired, eyes replaced and fine heads of hair restored.

The interior of that shop was a great disappointment to me when we went to buy my fairy-cycle - not a bed, not a ward, not a doctor or nurse in sight anywhere!

SPRING CLEANING

These two words were dreaded by all husbands and children, because they meant that everyday life must cease whilst the whole house was turned upside down. Mothers put away their knitting, sewing, crocheting, patchwork quilt-making, and changed from smiley personalities into fierce work-horses.

Everything washable was washed - curtains, bedding, table-linen, antimacassars, covers, treasured wedding presents such as dinner services, cut-glass vases, cruets, biscuit barrels, fancy tea-pots, china dogs etc. etc. Even the handles of scrubbing-brushes, sweeping-brushes, shovels and mops were attacked.

All drawers, cupboards, and cubby-holes were emptied and scrubbed out. They were then lined with newspaper, before precious objects were lovingly replaced. The most house-proud ladies lifted up the lino (or oil-cloth) in their bedrooms and scrubbed the wooden boards underneath!

Stair-matting and pegged rugs were slung over the clothes-line in the backyard and whacked unmercifully with a wicker carpet-beater by perspiring women with big, red-and-white-spotted handkerchief 'masks', tied cowboy-style across their faces, to protect their lungs from the swirling clouds of dust.

Stair-rods and fire-irons were polished with Brasso until they shone like gold. No corner of the house was left undisturbed. Whilst flock mattresses were off beds to receive attention, the wire springs were given a pleasant tickling with a feather-duster to remove any lurking particles of dust.

The only weapons in this annual battle against dirt were brushes for various purposes, dust-pans, mops, floor-cloths and dusters.

AUGUST BANK HOLIDAY

1. DAY TRIPPERS

Because workers were given only one week of annual leave, Bank Holidays were greatly appreciated, especially the first Monday in August. Day-trippers went off to the seaside, the Lakes, the country-side and to horse-races. Carnforth station was a very busy place with lots of excursion-trains stopping to drop off and collect passengers.

Children from the Hill Street area perched on the double-barred iron railing at the top of Stanley Street to observe the Bank Holiday traffic on the main road. With pencils and note-books, (or tea-packets turned inside out and carefully smoothed) boys liked to collect car registration number (TB for our area). Girls preferred to write down the pretty names of holiday charabancs, such as Blue-bell, Red Rose, White Lady and Silver Fern, etc.

During long gaps in the flow of traffic, the railings

were grand for us children to practise gymnastics. To contort oneself into a Flying Angel position showed a high degree of proficiency!

2. THE SPRING FIELD

In the afternoon, our neighbours assembled at the top of Stanley Street, carrying their wicker shopping baskets packed with food. Soon the strains of the Brass Band could be heard as they marched along Lancaster Road, and we joined the happy crowd on its way to the Spring Field for a communal picnic.

The band took up its position on the fat stretch of grass near the canal's stone-faced banking, used in the mid-1800s as a wharf, where coal was unloaded from horse-drawn canal barges.

Parents sat on their coats and enjoyed listening to popular tunes, whilst we children played ball or practised jumping over the little stream which bisected the field as it trickled down into the canal. It could have been crossed by a big, flat stone which formed a bridge, but that was considered boring! Several children, having fallen into the stream, ran crying to their parents, who gave them a sharp clout, not sympathy.

Young eyes peered curiously into the five mysterious 'caves' in the side of a grassy hillock nearby. "Keep out of there!" our parents would shout unnecessarily. The dark, smelly interiors did not invite exploration, because tramps used them as en-suite bedrooms with all conveniences at hand.

No one ever told us that they had been bee-hive type coke ovens. The oom-pa-paahs continued as baskets were unpacked and we enjoyed corned-beef sandwiches and jam-butties, washed down with sweet tea, drunk from the cups which screwed on to the top of thermos flasks. O, happy, happy day!

3. EXCURSIONS

High, old-fashioned Waggonettes, drawn by 2 horses, carried Morecambe holiday-makers on excursions to Silverdale. They stopped at our Station Hotel for high tea and, when they resumed their journey, Carnforth lads often clung to the steps at the back to get a free-lift. The long whip of the driver quickly whisked them off as if they were troublesome flies.

CARNFORTH NEWS ITEMS

- In Cragbank Lane, not far from the Travellers' Rest Beer House, the Toffs of our town played tennis on the courts there, or enjoyed a relaxing game of Croquet on the Green. Most working-class people, however, preferred to spend their spare-time more profitably by gardening or looking after some hens and a pig. The Gardeners' Association and The Poultry Club held annual shows in the Co-operative Hall.

Music-lovers joined Mr Unsworth's Choral Society and our intellectual inhabitants exercised their brains at the exclusive Chess Club.

- Great excitement! Harry Lauder, the famous Scottish entertainer, broke his train journey to London and made a brief, but memorable, visit to the Kinema. It is though that he stayed over-night at the Station Hotel.

- During the summer, a company of army territorials camped in Rocky Field, Cragbank (just over the railway bridge). Locals greatly enjoyed the Sports Day organised by the soldiers, and I won a small, glass rose-bowl for running.

- Fred, publican at the Cross Keys, was consulted about his excellence in the art of pig breeding. When asked what breed he preferred, he prefaced his answer with a phrase he used before all his remarks: "Like as though you know, them as 'as curly tails."

- Our famous Brass Band acquired a hut alongside the path which leads from the Kellet Road canal-bridge down to the Canal Cottages.

- Riggs, the Building Contractors, lived at Oxford House at the top of Oxford Street. The family owned one of the first private cars in Carnforth. Richard Moss was the driver (not quite as posh as a chauffeur.)

- Children beware! Within spitting distance of the Cross Keys lived no less than 2 headmasters and 4 teachers! Namely, Mr Cobbe and Mr R T Barnard, Mrs Garth (Annas Bank), Miss Garth (Bank Terrace) and the Misses Deborah and Josephine Wilkinson (Kellet Road).

- A Children's Ball in the Co-operative Hall in no way lived up to its name! When introduced to an open expanse of very slippery floor, the thoughts of a crowd of lively children did not automatically turn to stately ballroom dancing. If the Master of Ceremonies (M.C.) did not keep strict order, what could develop was: a) A scene of jolly skaters enjoying themselves on a frozen pond, or b) a tribe of a frenzied jungle-dwellers performing wild war dances around an imaginary camp-fire. It is not remembered that Gwen Cambray did a graceful valetta with Walter Rainford or that Lizzie Shaw waltzed with Jackie Wilson and Maisie Ashton with Norman Cresswell. We did, however, have an excellent dancer at our Sunday School events. He was a boy named Billy Turner, who lived down Grosvenor Place and was well-known locally for doing lovely Scottish dancing in full Highland dress.

[Billy's name was mentioned lately when I was

SHARED BACK-YARDS

At the top-end of Hill Street, each group of four adjacent houses shared one backyard. My home, number 13, shared with numbers 9, 11 and 15 and, one dark winter's night, death almost came amongst us.

On a grassy patch in front of our back door was a rectangular flat stone (approximately 20 in x 15 in) which featured in many childhood games - it could be a stage, a table for tea-parties or an altar for weddings.

An unruly lad who lived in Lower North Road managed, under cover of darkness, to prise up the stone which, unknown to anyone, was the cover for a deep well used in the days before Carnforth had tap-water.

A hasty dash across to one of the our earth closets, which stood in a row opposite houses numbers 9 and 11, could have meant an untimely exit from this world for one family member.

126

FEEDING BABIES

Most babies were fed on breast-milk - cheap, convenient and the cat couldn't get at it! Less fortunate ones were reared on Nestlé's Condensed Milk (delicious in sandwiches!). The diluted milk was poured into circular, flat-sided 'titty-bottles' with the teat at the end of a long, narrow tube - handy, but extremely unhygienic.

NEWS ITEMS

1. IRELAND

King George V proclaimed the existence of the Free State of Ireland, so Miss Taylor, our teacher in Standard I, was most definitely a foreigner.

2. THE BBC

Amazing! The first entertainment, a singer with musical accompaniment, was heard 'over the air' from Marconi's Chelmsford Broadcasting Station, in February. In October, the British Broadcasting Company was formed and, a month later, at 6pm on November 15th, the first regular news broadcast was made from a room in Marconi House in The Strand, London.

Most listeners had to use head-phones at first but, for the fortunate few, loudspeakers made it possible for whole families to listen together. It was now over 2 years since wireless had been proved possible with the broadcast of Dame Nellie Melba.

Now the BBC was planning to give listeners a diet of concerts, talks and news. John Reith had been appointed as General Manager.

This was something to which Carnforthians could look forward in the future, but sadly wonders of science took a long time to arrive Up North, and the cost could be beyond their means.

3. WAGES

To help in the economy drive, policemen had their wages pegged at £234 per year (£4.50 per week). Our townspeople gained confidence from seeing the local Mr Plod out on his beat, and voiced their approval when he boxed the ears of naughty children.

School teachers were also warned by the Government not to ask for any pay rises. Some people thought they were already overpaid, considering their long holidays.

TABLE TALK

When the evenings became cold and dark, children were happy to remain indoors and sit around that essential piece of furniture, a large sturdy-legged, square table which stood in the centre of most Carnforth living-rooms, near the comforting warmth of a coal fire.

By the light of a large oil-lamp in the middle of the table, the kiddies could play Ludo and Snakes-and-Ladders, read their books, draw, paint or cut out pictures from old papers and magazines. They sat on home-made wooden stools which nestled permanently under the table. To prevent its legs from being scratched, the table wore long-woollen stockings held up with elastic garters!

The table's white-wood top was protected with a piece of prettily-painted Lancaster Cloth, made locally at Williamson's Linoleum and Oilcloth factory, which could be seen, near the River Lune, from trains travelling over Carlisle Bridge.

The Lancaster-cloth with its fleecy backing was easy to wipe over, and saved on the laundering of big, white-linen table-clothes, which were only used on Sundays and for parties, when the two spare extensions leaves were pulled out so that a large family group could sit down to eat together.

Mothers spent many hours working on the white table-top. On Mondays, dry clothes were brought in from the washing-lines in the backyard and, on the table, each item was dampened with flicks of water from a quart jug before being carefully folded and placed in the wicker clothes-basket, ready for mangling. After that they were left over-night.

On Tuesdays, a pad of old blankets, topped with a piece of sheeting, was placed on the table ready for the ironing. The flat-irons were heated on the coal-fire, which had to be glowing, not flaming - not an easy arrangement because the flats tended to put the fire out whilst it, in return, made them black and sooty so that they had to be wiped frequently on a piece of old rag before use.

Wednesdays were baking days so out came the large earthen-ware mixing-bowl (brown on the outside and yellowish and very slippery inside), the weighing scales and the well-scrubbed baking board. Bread was mixed and left in the hearth to 'rise', whilst pastry was rolled-out for fruit pies, custard pies, currant-pasties, and dumplings. (Not owning a small tin bath, one Hill Street mother bathed her wee babe in her mixing-bowl. A difficult job as the tiny mite slid about like an elusive eel!)

On Sundays, the table stood serenely resplendent, wearing a read plush or chenille cloth with exciting bobbles around its edges. For good people, the Sabbath was a day for rest and Church-going.

CHRISTMAS-TIDE

The arrival of December meant the start of preparations for the most specials of the year's highlights: Christmas, eagerly anticipated and planned for well in advance.

When busy mothers were making the cake, the pudding and the mincemeat, children were always close by to lend helping (?) hands. All the dried fruit had to be washed and then dried on clean tea-towels (cup-towels, if your family once came from Yorkshire.) Extracting seeds from fat, luscious raisins was a fiddly job that the kiddies willingly volunteered to do, because they could surreptitiously keep popping one into their mouths.

Mixing bowls were passed round so that everyone could take a turn with the arduous stirring and mixing. That would bring good luck, said crafty mothers. There was no shortage of willing tongues to eventually clean out the bowls!

The nicest part of making the pudding was the stirring-in of tiny, silver charms, bought on a card from Wall's Toffee Shop at the top of Stanley Street. Oh, the thrill of finding one in your mouthful of pudding on Christmas Day - a little horse-shoe meant good luck, a wish-bone granted a wish, and a minute thimble foretold that you'd be an old maid (providing you were not already an old fellow!). No one in the family was ever stupid enough to swallow a charm.

A week or so before Christmas, armed with an empty sack, folk set off up one of Carnforth's pretty lanes, not to collect firewood this time, but to look for holly bushes, hopefully laden with berries.

People loved to have lots of pictures hanging by cords from big nails hammered into the walls of their rooms. Scenes from Bible stories and illuminated texts were favoured for bedrooms. Landscapes, seascapes and an abundance of family portraits beautified the walls of parlours and living-rooms and, for the festive season, a bunch of holly was propped behind each frame.

Using flour-paste, the children then spent happy

hours carefully linking together strips of coloured paper to form paper-chains which criss-crossed the room.

And so, 1922 reached its close.

1923

The merrymakers who had assembled on the Market Ground to welcome in 1923 were joined just before midnight by a jolly group of dancers, who had the backs of their hands stamped before leaving the NDFS New Year's Eve Ball (10pm to 2am) in the Co-operative Hall.

The National Deposit Friendly Society was a club, which eased the worry of medical expenses for its members and, for many years, its New Year's Eve Ball was to become an important annual event.

SHOPS

Our shops were important to Carnforth folk and, as valued customers, Carnforth folk were important to the shopkeepers. A welcoming chair stood by most counters.

1. WEDLAKES

'Wet-Legs', as it was known to us children, was a very prosperous newsagent business in a tin hut at the top of Haws Hill. The shop's proximity to the C of E School meant that it caught most of the pupils' trade. It specialised in an exciting variety of sweets to suck, to lick or to gnaw (tiger-nuts, woody liquorice sticks, and locust beans, which moo-cows also enjoyed). Huge gob-stoppers were taken out of the mouth repeatedly to observe how they magically changed colour. Some children were kind enough to allow their best friend to have a quick suck. We all thought that Cobblers' Wax was horrid, but we endured the taste because hidden inside were tiny, metal lucky-charms. It would have been stupid to swallow those! The whole of one's Saturday penny could be spent at one go, but nice things could be bought for ½d (an 'a'penny) or even ¼d (a farthing - 960 for £1). *[Cunliffes were the shop's next owners.]*

2. CARR'S

[Introducing the first mini-car in Carnforth]

Annie and Minnie Carr served in the shop on Lancaster Road owned by their father Robert, who was advertised in Bulmer's Directory of 1901 as a grocer and beer retailer. Children waited outside whilst Minnie was serving at the metal-topped, toffee counter on the right. Bad-tempered and vinegar-sour was that lady! She snatched sweets from the brass weighing scales before they had had time to balance, and merited her title of Skinny Minnie.

The door-bell gave a welcoming 'ping' as we children rushed in when Generous Annie, all smiley and kind, came on duty. In obedience to The Pledge we had made at the Band of Hope, our young eyes did not turn to the counter on the left-hand side of the shop, because there intoxicating liquor was sold.

We looked longingly at the shelf of toffees in large bottles - Thorne's nut-caramels, sugared almonds, mintoes - but at 4d per ¼lb they were far too expensive! After long deliberation, we made our choices from the open boxes displayed in the window. Dolly-mixtures, jelly-babies, rosy-lips, aniseed balls, blackberries and raspberries, love-hearts with soppy messages on them, sherbet-fountains, fizzy khali to make yellow drinks etc. etc. Food of the gods contained in cone-shaped paper bags!

3. THE CHIP SHOP

Folk queued up in my Uncle Arthur Barnham's busy chip shop in Market Street when the first and second houses 'let out' at the Kinema, at 8 and 10.30pm. "A tupp'ny fish, a pen'rth o' chips and a few scraps please," was a frequent order.

Potatoes were peeled by a clanking machine, which almost filled the backyard. Chips fell down into an enamel bucket when potatoes were placed, one by one, in a contraption with a heavy lever, which stood at one end of the shop counter.

Nothing could compare in taste with chips eaten outdoors from a vinegar-soaked newspaper wrapping!

Besides being a busy shopkeeper and housewife, my Auntie Maggie was mother to lively lads, Billy and Frank, and to twin babies, Mary and Arthur.

[Young-'uns don't know they're born these days!]

Uncle Arthur, paralysed in a leg and an arm, was a

familiar figure around Carnforth in his little trap drawn by Dolly the pony. His hobby was going to local sales and buying an amazing variety of secondhand objects which shocked Auntie Maggie, but delighted my cousins, e.g. a large metal disc, in a glass-fronted case, which produced wonderful tinkly music when wound-up.

4. THE FENT SHOP

Miss Thexton had a small fent shop on Lancaster Road near the Parish Church. There, ladies bought remnants of material and sewing requirements. In a large box near the door, she had lots of penny bundles of scrap materials known to little girls as 'doll-rags'. How they loved to root about in that box, and many were the happy hours they spent sewing Magyar dresses for their dolls.

DOWN MARKET STREET WAY

Thrifty mothers bought a sheep's head at Butcher Billy's, and then called in at little Mrs Dixon's Green-Grocer's shop lower down the street. There they bought the ingredients for a good, nourishing soup which was cooked in the set-boiler, carefully scrubbed out after washing-day. The fire in the small grate below could boil 5 or 6 gallons of water

Jackson's Café Shop was extra busy on Saturdays. A selection of small, delicious cakes could be bought, 13 for one shilling (260 for £1!), Everything they sold - bread, buns, scones, cakes etc. - was made in their Preston Street bake-house. In the café upstairs, cold luncheons were served and wedding receptions and funeral teas could be booked. In an evening, the room could be hired for small events.

The Lancaster Guardian reported that, at a whist drive organised by the NDFS, the prize was a Dorothy Bag. Besides serving behind the counter, Hilda Jackson (daughter of the owner) took huge wicker baskets full of supplies on to the station for the restaurant cars of express trains, which stopped here.

[Eventually she married one of the attendants.]

At Mrs Helliwell's Millinery Shop (No. 17) wedding and mourning orders were advertised as specialities, also dresses, gloves and veiling etc. Large-brimmed hats were held in place with fancy pins and veiling, which covered the face. One day I was to kiss my grandma and refused, saying, "Oh no, please, not until she lifts up her blind."

R J Lugsdin (No. 9 Telephone 29) was a Tailor and Ladies' and Gents' Clothier and Outfitter. Just the mention of this gentleman's name caused children to chuckle, for some reason or other. His long overcoat with an Astrakhan collar was reputed to know its way around Carnforth by itself. To adults he was known as 'Bobby Dear'.

In the Council Chambers Buildings (Upper Market Street), Miss Thompson ran a Penny Bazaar. She sold pots of all kinds, books and a wide variety of goods. She also ran a Penny Club for children's books at Christmas-time. 'The Chatterbox' was a firm favourite.

The Smalleys lived over their Chemist Shop at the top of the street, opposite the Co-op's 2 large departmental shops: the drapery and the furnishing. Children loved Smalley's shop window because of the 4 huge flasks full of beautifully coloured liquids, which shone like jewels - red, green, blue and yellow.

MOVING-UP AT SCHOOL

It was an important step up the education ladder at the C of E School when the Standard I children were ready to move upstairs.

My twin friends, Agnes and Walter Rainford, did not make the move, because the previous year they had left in order to attend the Roman Catholic School up Coulstan's Lane at Bolton-le-Sands, where they were taught by Miss Lazenby, possibly a lady of foreign origin.

I had considered becoming a Catholic myself when Agnes told me that, when she was confirmed (aged 7), she had been given an additional Christian name: Winifred - one of my favourites! I thought how lovely it would be to write Emerald, Goldie or Rosebud after Marion. When I realised that I'd have to say my prayers in Latin and also considered that long wearisome walk to Bolton-le-Sands every day, I decided to stay with the Protestant Faith. But I did like the Catholic priest,

Father Wilcox! His bright, smiling face and friendly manner won the respect of people of all faiths over a wide area.

On a memorable day in Spring, Miss Taylor marched us out of the Standard I, across the playground to Miss Pelter's classroom at the head of the stairs. We'd 'Gone Up' to Pelter-The-Belter in Standard II. Poor soul! She was no crabbier than the other teachers were.

The position of her classroom would have caused an angel to shed the feathers from its wings! All day long, her lessons were interrupted by a stream of clattering children from classes VII, VI, V, IV and III on their way to the closets in the two playgrounds, boys through the door on the left and girls to the right.

The school had neither corridors, hall nor staffroom! To make matters worse, Standards II and VII shared a classroom, separated only by a curtain. It was a wonder that Miss Pelter was able to teach us anything at all!

A PARLIAMENTARY ELECTION

Carnforth was very busy. It was Election Day and bright blue, yellow and red "Vote For ..." posters were on all the placards. There was a lot of activity at both the Conservative and Liberal Club rooms. The Labour Party in Britain was growing and Ramsay McDonald had been elected as the leader, so the Carnforth members were hopeful at their headquarters in a sitting-room in New Street. People were to-ing and fro-ing to the Church of England School where voting was taking place, so we scholars had been given a welcome holiday.

My mother, brought up as a Tory, had decorated my fairy-cycle with a mass of blue ribbons, bows, streamers and rosettes, and then very naughtily sent me on an errand to the home of my staunchly Liberal Grandma and Granddad Wilkinson in Grosvenor Place.

I was not given a loving welcome that morning!

The next day, my mother and I joined the crowd, assembled on the road in front of the Conservative Club in Station Buildings, as the election results were read out. Lord Balneil had won and he thanked everyone present from one of the Club's windows. Seeing him was a great disappointment for me because, instead of wearing a velvet, fur-trimmed robe and a gold coronet, he was dressed in an ordinary suit such as my dad wore on a Sunday!

SUMMER EVENINGS

On warm, summer evenings, the scene down Hill Street was like a Lowrie painting which had come to life: people relaxing on stools near their door-steps, children skipping in a long clothes-line being 'twined' by two obliging mothers, girls doing cork-work or stitching doll-clothes, boys swapping fag-cards, playing marbles or kicking a ball about, and an attentive group around Mr Gibbons, who was tootling merry tunes on his tin-whistle whilst sitting on an old kitchen chair outside his front door.

A man of many talents was Mr. Gibbons! He excelled at knitting. One of his creations was a complete outfit - hat, jumper, skirt, and stockings - in brown and orange stripes for his daughter Mary. He proudly held her hand as he led her down Carnforth's 'Cat Walk' to the shops. *["Oh dear!" she groaned to me many years later, "I felt like a *** wasp!"]*

Local craftswomen were quite shame-faced when that goods guard beat them all by winning the knitting-prize at Silverdale Exhibition with a lovely, dainty, pink and white bedspread.

A PRIZE-WINNER

We were very proud of any Hill-streeter who could win prizes and beat other townspeople.

One of our neighbours, a L.N.W.R. Goods Guard, was an expert at his job. Each year he won First Prize in a competition for coupling and uncoupling wagons in the marshalling yard.

The prize was a magnificent silver teapot, which could have stood on a white, crocheted d'oyley and graced anyone's mahogany sideboard. His wife, however, put the treasure into daily usage and kept it standing on the hob so that a cup that cheers was always ready at hand. Of course the inevitable happened eventually. A hole appeared in the sooty side of the lovely teapot. But heigh-oh! Not to worry. A new one could be won next year.

TIMBER!

Timber was one of Carnforth's local industries. At the top of Haws Hill was Steele's Saw-Mill, with its timber-yard running alongside The School Lane by Willow Cottage. Hundreds of huge logs were stacked there, making a death-trap for the adventurous children who climbed on top of the piles of those giants of the forest, and wriggled along between them.

It is not recalled that any of them was seriously hurt, but accidents did happen to the workers in the mill, where the huge circular saw whizzed, whined and scattered showers of sawdust. Steele's men could be identified when at the pub they ordered, "Five pints please," and displayed a hand with only two remaining fingers.

A DUSTY SKI-RUN

Workers carried sacks full of waste sawdust across the road in Haw Hill and tipped it down the banking into the Gravel Hole. This formed a thick, steep 'ski-run', down which children loved to race with whoops of joy. They landed at the bottom with pockets and footwear full of sawdust, which also clung to their hair, went down their necks, up their noses and into their ears.

Unfortunately, it was not nice clean sawdust, because Johnny Blackburn stabled his horse nearby and tossed rubbish from his cart down the slope. It was not unknown for the little girls to find a fish-head trapped up the legs of their knickers.

WHO'S DIED?

From our back bedroom window, we could see Rigg's Yard at the other side of a high wall. When, after working-hours, lights were seen on, and hollow hammering sounds echoed inside the big Joiners' Shop, neighbours in the locality wondered who had died - coffins were handmade from personal measurements.

WHAT A SIGHT!

Haws Hill Gravel Hole, formerly Tuer's Gravel Pit, presented a lunar landscape with its uneven hills and hollows. Hen-runs and pigsties occupied any available site.

It was separated from Haws Hill by a big, sturdy fence made of upright railway sleepers, with an entrance near The Haws where Mr Fletcher the chemist lived.

One day, a man, standing near the hoardings next to the Kinema and looking towards Haws Hill, was horrified to see a river of rats flowing towards him from the Gravel Hole. He was greatly relieved when the creatures turned left and streamed over the railway bridge, past the Post Office.

SPRING CLEANING AGAIN

Some husbands were cajoled into lending a hand with the annual Spring Clean. They went to Riggs' Yard at the bottom of Oxford Street with metal buckets to buy quick lime, to which they later added water and dolly-blue. A thick boiler-stick, used in the copper on wash-days, was used to stir the mixture, which was then applied by means of a wide, flat brush to all the ceilings in the house and to the walls of the back kitchen, the cellar and the earth closet in the back yard.

One's respectability was assessed from one's standard of cleanliness. Some lazy folks' closet were dirty, dark places, festooned with more lacy, grey cobwebs than a haunted house, whilst lurking in the corners were huge, hairy spiders the size of pan-lids!

PLAYING OUT

Street games came round in seasonal rotation. Suddenly it was marble-time, skipping-time, whip-and-top-time, bowler-time or hop-scotch-time etc. No one knew who set these 'times' off, but they quickly spread from street to street until all Carnforth children were happily playing the same game for a while.

To choose who would be the leader or chaser in any particular game, a procedure called 'dipping out' took place.

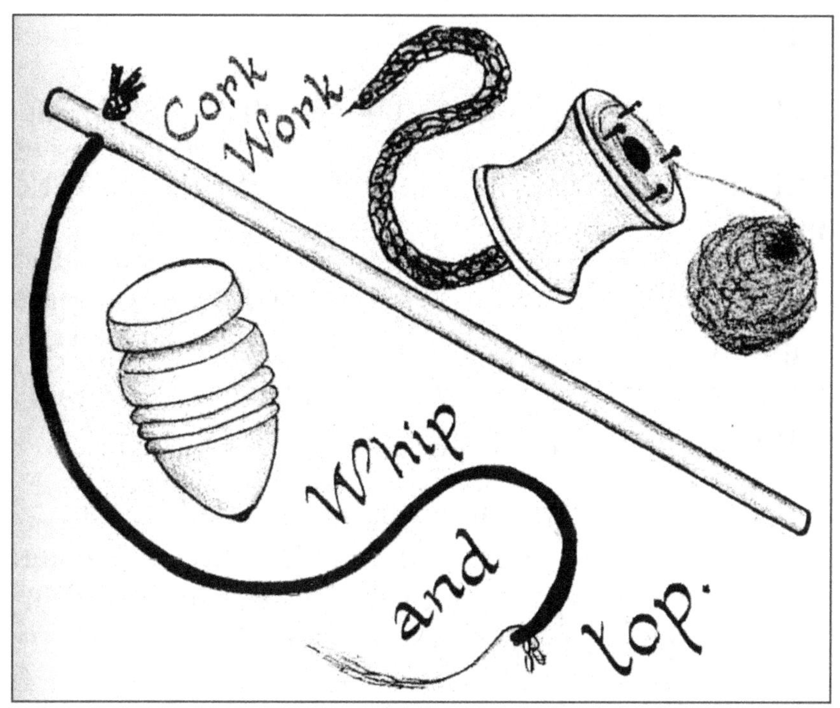

We stood in a tight circle and chanted weird incantations as a finger was pointed to each child in turn:

"Ickle ockle, black bottle. Ickle ockle, out!" Of course, our naughty boys could always supply a saucy version:

Λ) "Ecney, meany, miney mo, put the baby on the po. When it's done, wipe its b**. Eeney, meany, miney, mo."

B) "Inky-pinky pen and inky, I can smell an awful stinky, and it comes from y-o-u."

We had a wealth of rhymes to accompany skipping and ball exercises and any sneaky child would have to listen to:

"Tell tale tit, your tongue shall be split,

And all the doggies in the town will have a little bit."

Girls needed skill and stamina to sing as they skipped in groups in a long rope: "All in together girls, never mind the weather girls. O-U-T spells out! Pitch, patch, pepper!"

A girl's wedding arrangements could be foretold by her stumbles during one particular skipping song: Would she marry "A tinker, tailor, soldier, sailor, rich man, poor man, beggar-man, thief?"

Would her wedding gown be made of "Silk, satin, muslin, rags?"

Would she arrive at church in "A coach, carriage, wheel-barrow, muck-cart?"

And her future home be a "House, palace, pigsty, pettie?"

We chose to falter in only the best of places! The words of one skipping rhyme would no doubt cause the lifting of parental eye-brows:

"I like coffee, I like tea,

I like sitting on a black man's knee."

Street Games joyfully remembered are:

- Poor Mary sits a-weeping.

- In and out the windows.

- Roman Soldiers and Ancient Britons.

- Wallflower, wallflower growing up high.

- The big ship sails through the illy-ally-o.

- I sent a letter to my friend.

- The farmers' in his den *[Yes! Den NOT Dell!]*

- What time is it Mr Wolf?

- Statues. ('It' whizzed each girl around and flung her into space. The motionless statue with the most graceful arrangement of limbs was the winner).

Hill Street slopes gently down to the bottom-end and that proved to be an asset for some street games. 'Relievo' was a favourite winter-warmer, and so also was 'Bowling'. Girls patted wooden bowlers (hoops) with a stick, but boys preferred iron bowlers propelled by a hooked-on metal rod.

'Bladders' was most definitely a boys' game! Obtained from a butcher's shop, horrible blood-stained objects, which had been part of the insides of dead animals, were blown-up and tied on to sticks by sadistic boys, who chased defenceless girls in an attempt to biff them on the head. (It must be said that the girls actually enjoyed being chased!)

'Pavement Concerts' were very popular. A line-up of chorus girls, arms linked across shoulders, did spectacular high kicks as they sang, "I want to be happy, but I can't be happy till I make you happy too!"

The boys, enjoying the flash of lace-trimmed knickers, were very willing to provide the audience. They still refused, however, to be bridegrooms when another royal marriage made Wedding games popular again. Jimmy Taylor, Albert Cambray, Jackie Wilson, Norman Cresswell, William Howie and Walter Rainford all declined to play the part of Prince Albert, Duke of York, when he married Elizabeth Bowes-Lyon on April 23rd. Spencer Harmson, Jack Parkinson and impressively-named Delhi Murray were three big boys who would not deign to play with us at all, and neither would Gladys Parkinson, Ella Murray or Mollie Walkden.

The equipment for our games cost little, or nothing. For Hopscotch, we needed only a piece of shiny tile and some white chalk to mark out a rectangular shape with horizontal lines and a central cross, forming numbered sections into which we had to hop.

A small circle of leather, threaded on to a length of string, became a sucker after being dabbled into a puddle and pressed onto a stone. 'Who could transport the heaviest load?'

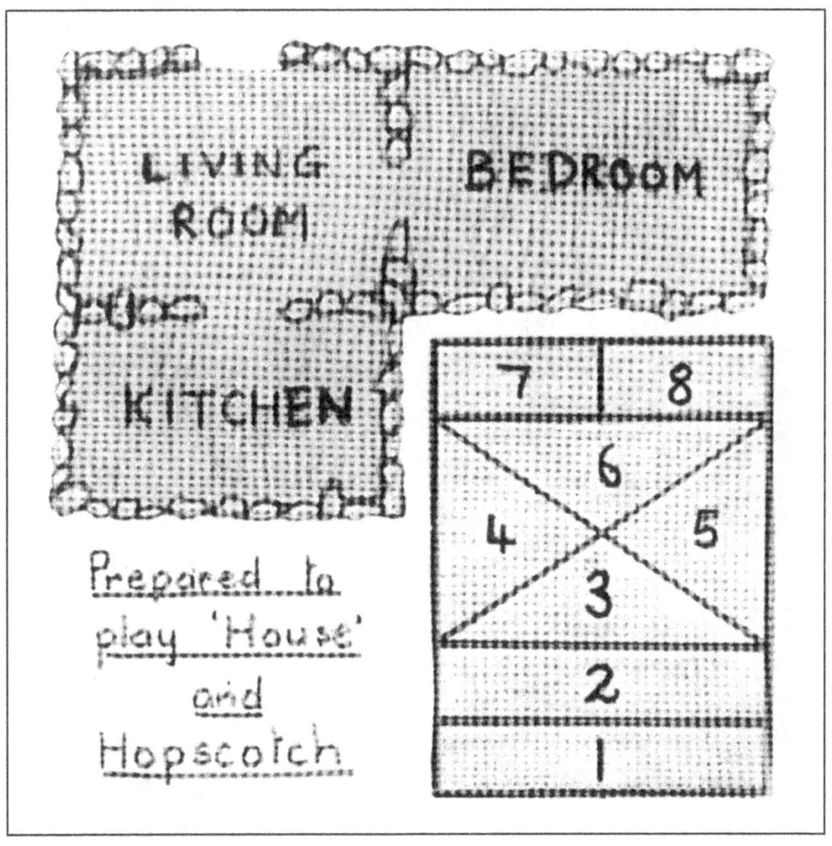

With a loop of string, friends played intriguing games of 'Cat's cradle', whilst another loop threaded through 2 holes knocked into a discarded tin-lid, made an exciting 'Whizzer' which, when humming at speed, could slice off the nose of anyone in its proximity. Balls, marbles and whips & tops could be bought for just a few coppers.

Girls always decorated their tops with coloured chalks and scraps of silver paper. Though poor financially, we were rich in ways to amuse ourselves!

Carnforth's various streets had their own favourite games. Popular in the Ramsden Street area, where boys seemed to outnumber girls, was 'Tin-Can Lurky', a game which combined can-kicking and hide-and-seek. 'Roaring Pipes' was great fun!

Stuffed up the down-sprouts of unfavourite neighbours were scrunched-up pages of newspaper, which were set alight. Flames and smoke shot up the drain-pipes and nearly scared the house occupants to death. 'Ducky Down' sounded a delightful game *[but its procedure is forgotten]*.

THE BAND OF HOPE

Thursday evenings were one of the week's highlights, because then children from all over Carnforth met in the Sunday-school room under the Wesleyan Chapel on Lancaster Road. There we enjoyed concerts or lantern slide-shows, which were designed to teach us about the dangers of alcohol and how over-indulgence would lead us into a life of misery. We were encouraged to 'Sign the Pledge' and promise to abstain from intoxicating liquor. I couldn't identify with any of it!

My dad was a member of The Sons of Temperance and a bottle of whisky lasted a long, long time, as it was kept strictly for medicinal purposes only at our house.

An article in the Lancaster Guardian, reporting on

one of the concerts, stated: "The splendid programme was arranged by the Misses E Chapman and L Hodgson. Lieut. Nicholson of the Salvation Army gave an address, which was listened to intently. A pianoforte solo was given by Ethel Ashton and recitations were given by Vera Letcher, Marie Wells, James Walkden, Marjorie Jackson and sisters Betty and Joan Wilkinson. Solos were sung by Beatrice Shaw and Marion Wilkinson." Me! With a voice like a corn-crake!

Wesleyan Young Leaguers (1927).
<u>Back row (left to right)</u>: Mrs Makinson, (3) Mrs Hindson, (4) Betty Sutton.
<u>Middle row</u>: (1) Ingleby, (2) Kerfoot, (3) Ethel Davies, (4) Beatrice Shaw, (6) me, (7) Beryl Byram.
<u>Front row</u>: (1) Rita Byram, (2) Shooter, (6) Jean Shooter, (8) Murray Parkinson.

Mrs. Edmondson was the person who kept order - "Quiet you Hill Street lot or out you go!"

[My friend, Beatrice Smith, recently informed me

that I sang, "I want a pie with a plum in. Don't want a mince-pie with rum in." I should hope not at a Band-of-Hope meeting!]

NEWS FROM ABROAD

- Adolf Hitler, a former corporal in the German Army, held his first public congress in Munich. The streets were full of flags and banners carrying the crooked-cross emblem of the swastika.

- Gabrielle "Coco" Chanel, the French fashion queen who had designed some of the most startling changes in women's appearance, decreed that even sweaters could be chic. She was leader in the trend towards a new freedom in clothes - straight boyish lines, short skirts, low heels, bobbed hair - designed to shake off the constriction of whale-bone.

STAYS

Despite fashion fads, married ladies in Carnforth still wore firm corsets (stays) with metal fastenings which snapped sharply into place at the front, whilst the back could be laced-up tightly to give the wearer a tiny waist.

Stockings - lisle in summer, woollen in winter - were held in place either by elastic garters, guaranteed to produce varicose veins in record time, or by metal suspenders, which dangled from the corset on lengths of elastic.

There was no restriction on bosoms, which were allowed to flop about and do their own thing. My mother sewed cotton bust-bodices for herself and, to ensure decorum, she wore dainty, laced-trimmed modesty vests in the neck of her dresses so that no male eyes would see any 'cleavage'.

HAIR

All the girls in my class at school had long hair. Although mine was as straight as a yard of pump-water, my mother was determined that I would have beautiful ringlets like the film star, Mary Pickford, who smiled sweetly from a long panel picture in our living-room. At bedtime, strands of my hair were wound tightly around curl rags - long strips of old sheeting. Oh, the pain of lying on those uncomfortable knobbles! I wished I could have had plaits like most of the girls.

All our mothers had long hair too, but they wore theirs in a bun. Long hair brought the problem of 'wick heads'. The ultimate disgrace would have been for a mother to be summoned to school because Nurse Nitty Nora the Head-explorer had discovered small game when carrying out her duty during a school medical examination, conducted by the school doctor with the fearsome name 'Tomb'.

To avoid such a humiliating experience, once a week, mothers made their daughters bend over a towel whilst their hair was given a good going-over with a fine toothed comb, commonly known as a bug rake. All debris falling on to the towel was closely scrutinised. Would some bits get up and walk about - "wick-uns" - or were they just eggs - "crackies" - which could be squashed between thumbnails? To keep troublesome head-lice at bay, hair was washed in a solution made from boiling water poured on to some quasher-chips which resembled wood-shavings.

For children bored with school lessons, adventurous 'wick-uns' could provide pleasant entertainment as they struggled up the complicated plait of a girl in the desk in front, or climb up a ringlet and then skid down the middle as though on a helter-skelter.

It was a brave 'wick-un' that chanced crossing the scalp of a lad whose hair had been styled by his dad, closely clipped all over the head with just a tufty fringe left at the front. A bang with a ruler by the boy in the desk behind would quickly terminate its life!

Carnforth did not have a ladies' hairdresser's. It did not need one. Hair was washed at home with soap, and given a gloss by adding vinegar to the jug of rinsing water. As a special treat on a wet day, nice, soft rainwater was collected in an enamel bowl.

Some ladies liked to have a pretty bunch of frizzy hair at each side of their faces, so they plunged a pair of curling-tongs into the red-hot coals of the open fire. If there was an odd smell of burning when hair was wound round them, and just a grey fizzled substance clung to them, then the tongs had been too hot, and should have been tested first on some paper.

A young lady who lived near us loved to go dancing on Morecambe pier. Under no circumstances could she take off her smart hat, because the pretty bunches of hair which framed her face were firmly stitched to her headgear.

HIGHFIELD TERRACE AND FAIRS

To enjoy ball-games, local children crept through gaps in the hedge which separated Highfield Terrace from the farmland in front of it. At the top of the field, a friendly horse, in hopes of some tasty tit-bits, looked over the five-barred gate which opened on to Kellet Road.

Highfield Terrace folk had a grandstand view when, on occasions, a travelling fair was set up in 'their' field. There were two other suitable sites: the Market Ground and the spare land down by the canal, near the Kellet Road canal bridge.

What excitement and fun those fairs brought to Carnforth! Large crowds assembled, attracted by the bright naphtha lights, and the blare of mechanical music from the steam organ in the centre of a big roundabout, with its flaring-nostrilled hobby-horses going up and down on shiny brass poles, twisted like sticks of barley-sugar.

Not everyone living nearby enjoyed the noise of a fair - the screams of the riders in the swing-boats, the oohs and aahs from the hoopla stall, the ping of bullets hitting the targets in the shooting gallery, the thud of wooden balls aimed at coconuts which seemed to have been glued on to their stands.

Next morning, when the caravans had moved off to pastures new, all that remained on the empty site were areas of flattened grass, mud and heaps of 'coddies' - rich manure for local gardens, donated by the caravan horses.

NATIONAL NEWS

1. A bill was passed to allow wives to divorce their husbands. This put the sexes on an even footing, and the wives of Carnforth's railwaymen warned their hubbies that there'd better not be any funny business when they were away from home "booking-off".

2. Members of Carnforth Cricket Club were loud in their praise of Jack Hobbs when he scored his 100th century in first-class cricket.

3. Wives hoped that the wireless would soon come to Carnforth when they read that new studios, opened at Savoy Hill by the BBC, would broadcast a programme called 'Woman's Hour'. There was a snag however, a wireless licence costing 10 shillings [50p]

would have to be paid for!

4. The motoring boom was opening up the countryside to a new breed of visitors. The Minister of Transport condemned unsightly hoardings and advertisements along the sides of roads. Our council would need to see that Carnforth's beautiful countryside was not disfigured. (Carnforth Motor Company, 5 and 7 Scotland Road, had a fine showroom, and a splendid Landau and a touring coupe for hire to our local visitors.)

5. Carnforth's three railway lines - the L.N.W.R., the Midland and the Furness - became part of the L.M.S., and the London Midland and Scottish Railway.

CHRISTMAS ONCE AGAIN

With holly behind the pictures and paper chains across the rooms, thoughts turned to Christmas trees. Shortage of space was a problem in crowded homes, so some 'natty' mothers' solution to that was to make a kissing bush: a seasonal mobile which could be suspended from the ceiling. Two play-hoops, pushed crosswise one into the other and secured with string, were covered with long lengths of coloured crêpe paper. The mobile was then decorated with sprigs of holly, mistletoe, lengths of tinsel and some shiny baubles unearthed from a dusty newspaper parcel on top of the wardrobe.

It was hoped that Father Christmas had not signed
The Pledge, and so would be able to enjoy the glass
of wine and a mince pie left out in readiness for
him.

1924

The NDFS New Year's Eve Fancy Dress Ball is remembered because, dressed in a homemade jester's costume with jingly bells on its pointy bits, I heard a woman snap at my mother, "For heaven's sake keep that d*** kid still. She's driving us made wi' them b*** bells!"

Mr Jim Archer, secretary of the National Deposit Friendly Society, lived at 69 North Road, next door to his relatives, the Dodsons, who were hard-working committee members.

WHIST DRIVES

These were a very popular form of entertainment, and the huge New Year Whist Drive which was held in the Co-operative Hall was a great success. Card tables covered the whole of the floor and overflowed onto the stage.

Folk took their Whist very seriously, and were eager to win one of the valuable prizes. Black looks were directed at any player 'throwing away' a trick. Pearson Wood, (father of Dorothy and Betty) who lived at 1 Haws Hill, was in great demand as a Master of Ceremonies. His sharp eyes could tot up the figures on winning score-cards at an amazing speed, and ensure that no 'reneging' had gone on.

THE LABOUR PARTY

An election in January caused much activity in our

town. It was a great day for the Labour Party. James Ramsay McDonald became the very first Labour Prime Minister to hold office. Labour was not in full power, however, because it needed the support of the Liberal Party. McDonald accepted the gift of a Daimler and £30,000 worth of shares in the biscuit firm McVitie and Price. Income from the shares paid for the running of the car for the rest of his life. The benefactor, who became a Lord, believed that every Prime Minister ought to have a car! Fiery, red-headed Ellen Wilkinson, a champion of women's rights, became a cabinet member.

EASTER

The approach of Spring-time and Easter inspired our local hens to produce a plentiful supply of eggs. Mothers chose some with strong-looking shells to convert into pace eggs by dyeing them pretty colours whilst they were being hard-boiled. Cochineal (beetles' blood - ugh!) produced shades of pink. Onion skins were the most popular dye because, wrapped around the eggs and held in place by a piece of old material, they made beautifully variegated patterns in yellow and brown. Names written on the eggs with candle-wax would magically appear after the dyeing process.

Down each street there was keen competition to see which family could have the most splendid display of pace eggs across the middle ledge of the sash-window in the front room.

Each district in Carnforth had its own Easter Field.

Ours was the Spring Field with a steep slope which was excellent for egg-rolling. Some folk believed that the custom was in memory of the stone being rolled away from the entrance to the tomb where Jesus was buried.

RAILWAY PERKS

Free passes and privilege tickets (¼ fare) were concessions granted to railway employees. My parents made good use of Dad's annual pass by going on holiday every year to places spread widely around Britain - Aberdeen, Edinburgh, Llandudno, Portrush, Yarmouth, Bournemouth etc. We went to London to visit the wonderful British Empire Exhibition which was held in Wembley. I remember a statue of the Prince of Wales made of butter, and a Wild West Show of bucking horses - a rodeo.

Children of large families, whose fathers were unemployed, were never taken on holiday. To them, a trip to Morecambe was a treat. They walked to Hest Bank on the canal banks, along by-ways to Bare and then along the promenade. Eating a pennyworth of periwinkles with a pin whilst dangling feet in the tide was a real delight. *[The coastal road had not been built.]*

AN ANCIENT BUILDING

The old Public Hall, next to the Shovel Inn and facing down Miller's Hall, had been superseded by the splendid Co-operative Hall in New Street, where all Carnforth's large social events were held.

The Public Hall was now used for furniture sales, when someone's home was broken-up, and for passing trade such as Lino Sales and Pot Fairs.

If customers were disloyal to our Co-op and purchased cheap oil-cloth there, it served them right when the modern pattern soon wore off, revealing a dowdy old design underneath. It was a temptation, however, to buy a bit of oil-cloth for up your back-passage for sixpence!

Doris Dinsdale *[as was]* went to a Pot Fair with her mother, who bought, at a remarkably cheap price, a job-lot of pots which included one of those essentials: a chamber pot. It would have been embarrassing to carry that unwrapped object to their home in Canal Cottages, so little brother Walter was persuaded to push it under his jersey.

SCHOOL TIME

At 8.50am, the bell on top of the C of E School rang-out to warn children that it was time they were on their way to school. The clatter of clogs was then heard all over Carnforth. Children had to race through the school gates before the second bell stopped ringing at exactly 9am.

Late-comers were locked out and had to wait on the landings, at the top of the boys' and girls' staircases, until Morning Prayers were over. Then it was 'line up for the cane' by the headmaster's desk, which was on a low platform in Standard III - the corner-room in the L shaped building. Nearby stood the piano, and all the glass partition-windows between the rooms were opened each morning so that the children in all 6 classes could join in with the hymns and prayers at Assembly Time.

Punctuality and regular attendance were very important factors instilled into scholars. A child felt very honoured to be allowed to ring the school bell by pulling a rope which dangled from the ceiling near Headmaster Cobbe's desk. Close by on the wall was a chalk-board, where the number of children present was marked-up after registration each morning and afternoon - approximately 220.

Children, sitting erect in their desks with arms folded, answered, "Present, Miss," as their names were called out from the class register. Actually the teacher in Standard III was a Mrs, not a Miss. This was very unusual because all lady teachers were compelled to leave if they got married. Probably Mrs Boak was a widow. I thought she was a very, very old lady.

[Later in life I learnt that she was 39 at the time!]

A banner was awarded to the class with the best attendance during the week. As a reward, its pupils were allowed to go home early on the Friday afternoon, and they were proud to have the banner on display in their classroom for the following week.

The Attendance Officer, named Mr Danson, called at school each week to take the names and addresses of any child who had been absent without a justifiable reason. This was to check that they were neither playing truant nor being kept at home to help their parents. His knock at one's door was feared as much as that of a policeman's.

ON A MUSICAL NOTE

To keep up with the Jones's, one had to have a piano! Two determined and stalwart ladies, my mother and our neighbour Mrs Ashton (barely 5ft tall), transported a beautiful second-hand piano from a local village to 13 Hill Street on a hand-cart. What a feat of strength and endurance! It was well worth the effort though - a fine rosewood instrument with an iron frame and a lovely front, inlaid with mother-of-pearl. My mother removed the ornate candle-holders which were not necessary because we had recently had gas installed to illuminate our living-room. Our horse-hair sofa was sacrificed to make room for the piano.

It was decided that Mr John Rigg, who lived at 'Meresbeck', where once my mother was in service, would be my music teacher. A lady called Miss Carter taught some local children, but was reputed to be rather strict. Smallwood's Pianoforte Tutor was widely used to help pupils to become musicians. Its tunes could be heard ringing forth from many front rooms - the plaintive plea of

"Won't you buy my pretty flowers?" the livelier "Bluebells of Scotland" and "Carnival of Venice", not forgetting the solemn sound of the hymn "Son of my Soul, my Saviour Dear."

Not all piano owners learnt to read music, but most children could play "I like chocolate" and "O! Can you wash your Father's Shirt?" The latter was cleverly played solely on the black notes, and with dramatic crossing of hands.

Lots of whistling was heard around our streets from errand-boys on heavy trade bikes, newspaper boys on their rounds, and knockers-up on their way to homes of railwaymen.

Sheets of musical medleys could be bought for 6d at Tomlinson's shop in Lancaster or from a stall in the covered market. There was very little canned music around, although a few better-off families in Carnforth had gramophones, which needed to be wound up and produced music from a large, bell-shaped horn.

IN LOVING MEMORY

There was still no burial ground in Carnforth, so the Sunday afternoon walks of many people took them across Warton Fields with bunches of flowers for the graves of relatives there. Some folk, who were unable to make frequent visits to the churchyard, bought wreaths made up of delicate white porcelain flowers, leaves and doves, protected under a glass dome.

I once found a wreath with a broken dome on the rubbish heap, and placed it on a tiny baby's grave which I had tended for many years. Lifting up the wreath one Sunday, I jumped back in horror to see a large brown snake coiled under it. From that day on I disliked artificial wreaths ... and snakes!

AROUND TOWN

1. 44 more Council Houses were built on an oval layout. King's Drive and Queen's Drive extended the nucleus of a large housing estate, which had started with the 8 houses in Prince Avenue - 328 houses were planned.

2. Carnforth's Water Company stated that our water supply was good and pure. The gathering ground for the reservoir at Withnets was of a peaty and sandstone nature, so the water was not hard. Arrangements had been made with the Manchester Corporation to obtain supplies from Thirlmere, if required.

3. The price of petrol at Greenland's Garage was raised to 2 shillings per gallon. Car manufacturers feared that this might deter many people from buying the new popular-priced small cars. A Morris Cowley cost about £175.

4. After a bazaar in the Church Room in Preston Street, there was a competition to see who could light the most candles with one match.

The winner lit 19. Every house had a candle-holder for trips down the cellar and to light the way to bed.

5. Holding hands and walking two-by-two, the children from the C of E School were led along beside the main road to the church, where special services were held on important days in the Church Year. On the way, some naughty children slipped into Carr's Toffee Shop and spent their penny collection money.

6. Co-op customers grumbled when they went to the Confectionary Department and found that the price of a 4lb loaf had gone up by ½d to 8½d. The increase was due to a dock strike.

7. The Lambsfield Motor Company was running an excellent service of red buses from Lancaster - Kendal and Lancaster - Carnforth - Warton, calling at intervening villages. When the blue buses of Fahy's Garage in Morecambe started up in opposition, children watching the traffic chose their favourites. Reds versus Blues. Goodies and Baddies. They cheered the buses on their side and booed the enemy's.

8. "If you want a glove for the foot," said the advertisement, "visit R Hunter, Foot Specialist. Repairs, Hand-sewn work done. Shop at the corner of New Street and Preston

Street."

9. Shrimp girl Mary, from Bolton-le-Sands, came regularly selling her wares from a wicker-basket. A spotless white cloth covered the shrimps which had been caught by her father in Morecambe Bay, and painstakingly 'picked' by pleasant, smiley Mary.

10. Our town still had a few 'Parlour shops' - hangovers from the Victorian Era, when poor wives had as few as half a dozen articles for sale displayed on their side-boards. "Plor" Rogerson had such a shop in his home down New Street, near Himsworth's excellent grocery shop. He sold 'Spanish' novelties at three for ½d, tobacco at 9d per oz and black twist, which he measured by winding it round his hand.

11. Carnforth Motor Co. specialised in the sale of new cars, commercial vehicles and motorcycles. It had a fleet of 6 open and closed cars for hire and good showrooms with courteous staff.

12. A colourful character, known as Rajah Whalli, came round Carnforth selling dainty handkerchiefs and pretty scarves from his suit-case. This glamorous, turbaned gentleman set many female hearts aflutter.

13. More romantic fantasies! The Prince of

Wales announced that he was going to start looking for a bride. Instead of flying through Carnforth station, why couldn't the Royal Train halt for a while, so that the heir to the throne could take a look at all the gorgeous girls who worked at Morphy's Sewing Mill?

14. In its brochure, Carnforth was proud to report that our town was clean and well-built. Because of its proximity to the sea, our air was pure and salubrious. Dr Jackson, our local Medical Officer of Health, announced that our health statistics were most satisfactory. The death-rate was very low, proving the healthfulness of Carnforth.

15. One Saturday night, little Jim Russell was in screaming pain with toothache. In desperation, his dad took him to Robin Hill surgery, only to find that both Dr Jackson and his son Dr Edward were out. Very obligingly, son Billy, who had failed his medical examinations, volunteered to pull out the offending tooth. He did so, and at the same time almost removed the unfortunate boy's jaw-bone.

FOOTBALL CRAZY

Our townspeople were strong supporters of the local team, 'Carnforth Rangers', which played on a field near Hagg Farm.

Remarkable scenes of enthusiasm were displayed

Our famous Carnforth Rangers.
<u>Back row (left to right)</u>: (3) Turk Byram, (4) G Cox, (5) Billy Byram.
<u>Middle row</u>: (1) Gordon Murray, (2) Wildman, (3) Billy Woods, (4) Bob Jackson (Plumber), 5 Speight, (7) W Bagguley.
<u>Front row</u>: (3) Johnny Wood.

on Good Friday when the players travelled to Morecambe to take part in the Infirmary Cup Final. The Brass Band played to a large crowd, assembled in the railway station forecourt to await a Special Train which had been booked to carry the excited supporters, the team and the band. A long queue had to wait at the booking office to gain access to the station where the train stood in Bay II of Platform One. Mr John Lindsay, without whose presence no football crowd was complete, sold rosettes, ticklers and other novelties in red and white (the team's colours) as he moved among the crowd.

The Lancaster Guardian reported that Miss Marion

Wilkinson, the Rangers' Mascot, caused much merriment when she led her team on to the field clad "in busby with quaint attire of red and white" *[actually I was in fancy dress as the Toy Drum Major - a popular song.]*

The Rangers won the cup and were given a rousing welcome at the station on their return. Crowds of happy supporters stood outside the Station Hotel and The Cup, full of good cheer and frisky germs, was passed from mouth to mouth.

Among the players, who helped our Rangers to win 3 cups during the season, were 'Turk Byram, Bily Bagguley, Bill Wood, Johnny Wood and Sid Parkinson (who later had a son named Cecil!).

PLAY GROUNDS

Each group of streets had its own playing-out area. Ours, strangely named "Butchers", was a rectangular piece of spare ground bordered by Hill Street backs, King Street backs, Alexandra Road fronts and the canal. The lower part, near the canal, was a rough area where tall spiky weeds and tangled undergrowth flourished, and that made it wild country, ideal for battles between Cowboys and Indians, Cops and Robbers, Britishers and Germans. The ammunition was berries shot through the hollow stems of a very tall weed (hemlock?).

The short grass at the top end of "Butchers" made it an excellent place for energetic games of football and cricket, and also for marbles and guinea-pig (a short piece of wood, balanced on a stone, was struck by a heavy stick and hit again whilst airborne).

'House' and 'shop' were games played mostly by girls, and necessitated a great deal of preparatory work. Lots of small stones had to be collected to lay out a house like an architect's plan, with spaces left for doorways. Dandelions in tin cans beautified the various rooms. Boys wouldn't play properly and kept stepping over our imaginary walls until some girl would shout, "Clear off t'work! You're allus under us feet!" (Just like a real wife!)

A lot of foraging around had to be done before a shop could be started up. Old kettles, pans and cans were wonderful finds, and so were flat tins which had once contained Mansion Polish, Zambuk, Cherry Blossom, Boot Polish, Gibb's Dentifrice or Brilliantine etc. These were used to display our stocks of flour (sand), sugar (broken glass), peas (small pebbles), flat toffee (broken brown pottery) and "bacca" (knobbly seeds of the weed plantain). Water from puddles, when added to soil and stirred with a twig, made delightful 'paddiwack'-butter which could be spread on leaves.

The disappointing part of this enjoyable game was that there was an abundance of busy shop-keepers, but a lack of customers. Buying was boring! A superb site for a shop was on the roof of one of Hill

Street's earth-closets.

Our mothers were not worried about our safety whilst we played happily on "Butchers". There was no vandalism and all our fun was free, until we heard the bell of the ice-cream man and raced home for money from mum for a ½d cornet, a 1d wafer or a pennyworth in a cup.

Happy, Carefree Days!

A TRIP TO THE SEA-SIDE

During the warm summer weather, our Hill Street Gang loved to go to that part of our shore known as The Rocks. With some jam butties wrapped in newspaper and bottles of water deliciously flavoured with lemon crystals, we set off to Cragbank through the fields and then along Shore Lane, fragrantly perfumed with honey-suckle and wild roses. Skylarks sang and all seemed peaceful, but dangerous, invisible germs might be lurking about The Cottage Hospital near the road-side, so we raced by on velvet tip-toes.

Approaching Marsh Cottages, we turned left and walked across the long meadow to the gate which opened on to Marsh Farm overlooking Carnforth Shore - no promenade, no pier, just a grassy foreshore with some scattered rocks, many small pools, and the River Keer winding its way across the mud flats of the estuary to the waters of Morecambe Bay. Across the river was the unattractive view of a long, low hill formed by deposits of slag from the furnaces of the Iron Works. Nevertheless, the sparkle of sunshine on water, the tang of salty sea-air and the call of sea-birds still made it the seaside for us, especially when the tide came up. With frocks tucked into our knickers or breeches' legs turned up, we loved paddling in the water, and tried to restrain ourselves from splashing about too much. We stamped on 'quick-sands' till they became dangerously wobbly, caught crabs in little pools, and collected a fleshy plant called Samphire for our mothers to pickle.

Welcome refreshment was found on the long, exhausting trek home at a well behind Mingins Farm, near Gragbank Green. Crystal-clear water was eagerly drunk from cupped hands. Seaside treasures taken home did not include any strange brown objects which had been seen floating along in the Keer. We felt sure they were not a rare form of sea-weed!

ANOTHER SEASIDE OUTING

One day, Mrs Smith, blessed with 14 fine children, and mother of my school friend Beattie, took her brood for a trip to Morecambe on the train. Whilst they were all waiting to be served in a chip shop, the smiling chappie behind the counter said, "Hello Mrs! Is this a Sunday School outing you have with you today?" "Indeed no!" answered Mrs Smith, giving him a withering glance. She announced very proudly, "They are all mine!"

[Thank you 'Beat' (now Mrs Wallace) for that fond memory. When I came to play with you, all those years ago, I was amazed to find your home brightly lit by electricity. Your dad worked wonders with that little engine in your backyard.]

THE WAR MEMORIAL

Many families in Carnforth were still grieving for the husbands, sons, fathers and brothers who had died overseas during the war, and so had no graves here. It was felt strongly that our town should erect a fitting memorial in honour of those whose lives had been lost, and a decision was reached that the statue of a solider should be placed in A Garden of Remembrance on the Market Ground, and the mammoth effort of raising £1,000 to finance the venture was begun. A fund-raising committee of 37 persons was appointed, headed by our nine councillors: F W Lambert, W R Williams, J Smalley, R T Barnard, J Murray, R Ashworth, J Kew, A E Linnell and Miss Willis.

THEIR NAME LIVETH FOR EVERMORE

Robert Abbot, Albert Armer, William Atkinson, John Baines, Samuel Balderson, Thomas Balderson, Robert Barton, Herbert Beattie, Ernest Beck, James Beclett, Thomas Bedford, Noel Bennet, Robert Broadbank, Fred Bullough, John Campbell, David Clark, James Clark, Thomas Capstick, James Disberry, John Edmondson, G Frederick Fleming, Harry Gardner, William Gilbert, William Glaister, Edgar Hall, John Harper, Harry Higginson, Morris King, James Kirkby, Richard Little, Percy Macefield, Christopher Marshall, George Morley, George Nelson, Edwin Parkinson, William Pedder, Herbert Penrith, Edwin Penswick, Harry Radcliffe, W Arthur Rigg, William Shaw, R Sidney Simpson, James Walkden, Edward Watson, John Watson, George Watson, William Whiteside.

A team of 27 collectors took on the task of calling at each house in Carnforth, collecting boxes were placed in all strategic positions, and every church, club and society joined in enthusiastically. Many individuals were filled with the desire to make their own special contributions. Down Hill Street, little Mrs Ashton boiled mushy peas in their thousands to sell by the basinful. She didn't feel she'd "Done her bit for the lads" until neighbours near and far were "Full up to here" with peas.

On September 5th, the War Memorial Fund published a small pink booklet entitled 'List of Subscribers', with the amount of the donation by each name, e.g. Mr J Kew had collected £9 2s 6d from 15 homes in Haws Hill and Booth Street, and had received sums of less than 5s, which came to £1 7s 6d - £10 10s in all.

The grand total for the whole of Carnforth was £891 7s 5d.

Our old Market Ground was chosen as the site for the Memorial because of its central position, and for the fact that it had always been the meeting-point for all our town's events. It was an uncared-for piece of land, and lines of flapping washing, overflowing from Hunter Street and Ramsden Street backyards, gave it an unsightly appearance.

Standing in the Garden of Remembrance, our Solider Monument was unveiled by Lord Richard Cavendish at 3pm on November 9th.

Unveiling of the Monument by Lord Richard Cavendish on November 9th, 1924. Background left, Cameraman at work. On the right the large sliding stone.

The dedication service was led by Reverend E Charlesworth and volleys were fired by soldiers of the 5th King's Own Regiment.

The names of Carnforth's 47 servicemen, who had died for our country, were recorded on plaques on the sides of the Monument.

Sadly they had no graves in Britain, but now they could be quietly remembered in the small pleasant park provided by our townsfolk.

BACK TO SCHOOL

Miss Deborah Wilkinson and Miss Alice Moore were the unfortunate teachers of Standards IV and V, who shared a large classroom, separated only by

Council School 1926

Back row (left to right): (1) E Watkins, (2) T Evans, (3) J Bainbridge, (4) J McDonald, (5) R Hodgson, (6) J Miller, (7) T Simpson, (8) T Hindson, (9) R Thexton, (10) H Taylor, (11) M Parkinson.
Middle row: (1) M Makinson, (2) J Carey, (3) R Hind, (4) H Forder, (5) M Craig, (6) D Bramall, (7) J Hodgson, (8) M Hind, (9) E Wilson, (10) B Byram.
Front row: (1) A Smith, (2) E Taylor, (3) G Cottam, (4) N Parker, (5) P Winter, (6) M Proudlove, (7) A Edwards, (8) G Smith, (9) N Swithenbank, (10) V Haslam.

a curtain.

After Morning Prayers, at which we always seemed to sing the same 5 hymns in the same order, (Mondays: "New Every Morning", Tuesdays: "Jerusalem the Golden", Wednesdays: "Jesu, Lover of my Soul" etc. etc.). We had Scripture Lessons and chanted strings of words which conveyed nothing to us. The Reverend Mercer came at regular intervals to test our knowledge of the Catechism and The Creed. He was a pious, solemn gentleman and would have fallen into a dead faint if he'd seen the inside covers of some of our History and Geography text-books. Naughty boys had written some very rude words in them ... with illustrations!

Arithmetic lessons meant memorising more and more Tables, so that we could eventually learn to do sums with £ - s - d, yds - ft - ins, lbs - ozs, miles - furlongs - chains, tons - cwts - stones, and so on.

Then there were HCFs, LCMs, long division, multiplication by factors, and tiresome Bills with long lists of requirements for awkward folk who wanted, for example 2¾yds of material costing 1s 11¾d per yd, or half a gross of apples at 10½d per doz.

'Grammar' turned out not to be a nice female relative, but a confusion of nouns, adjectives, verbs, conjunctions, adverbs, prepositions, objects, predicates and subjects. All made difficult to understand because, whilst teacher was explaining, naughty Freddie Mawson was using his ruler to flick inky blotting-paper-balls at Laura Moorby, Jack Astly was tying Freda Taylor's lovely curls to the back of her seat, and Robert Jackson was dipping Kathy Owen's long hair into his inkwell.

To be caught misbehaving meant being sent to Mr Cobbe's desk for a lash or two of the cane, which stung like a venomous snake. Spitting on palms beforehand did not ease the pain, and snatching your hand away as the cane was descending meant a double dose.

Young scholars at the posh 'new' Council School (1929?)
<u>Front row (nearest camera)</u>: Dorothy Stockton,
<u>2nd row</u>: Doris Whiteside, Maisie Moorby,
<u>3rd row</u>: Sammy Wilson, Hilda Worthington,
<u>4th row</u>: Billy Dawson, June Cook.
<u>Standing</u>: Doreen Tyson, Renee Cambray, Victor Parkin,
John Barket, unknown.

As a reward for good behaviour, it was grand to be chosen as a monitor. You could then get at those classmates, with whom you were out of friends, by giving them repulsive pens with chewed-up ends and nasty cross-legged nibs which couldn't write properly and sprayed blots all over one's page. New nibs issued by teacher shone like gold, but faced a hard life when used to poke patterns in blotting-paper, to stab fiercely into inkwells or fire like arrows into the floor. I used wet blotting-paper to keep my nibs and ink-wells clean and shiny. *[I do hope I didn't use spit!]*

The best thing about Singing Lessons was the fact that we could allow a great deal of noise to come out of our mouths without fear of punishment. With a map-pole, teacher pointed at random to notes of the tonic-sol-fah on a long narrow chart called a modulator, and hopefully we produced the correct sounds. What a row - about as harmonious as a bunch of disgruntled donkeys braying on Morecambe shore! The only song I recall singing was a dreary tune with endless verses entitled, "Dashing Away With The Smoothing Iron."

Botany lessons were mainly concerned with recognising the leaves of different trees and identifying the beautiful wild flowers which grew in profusion around Carnforth: king-cups and yellow flag from the canal-side near the Spring Field, shy little violets from Walker's Lane near Cockle Hall Farm, and lots of bluebells, primroses, cowslips and red campions from hedgerows not far from our homes.

We were given pot palettes with a squeeze of red, yellow and blue paint in their 3 sections so that we could colour drawings of our botanical specimens. When monitors gave out brushes, we hoped we wouldn't be given balding old things with only 3 or 4 bristles remaining.

Our Upstairs school had no water laid on! It had to be carried up from the small downstairs cloakroom under the stairs. Woe betide any scholar who fidgeted about and knocked over a jar of water. Something new and interesting was introduced into our educational lives in Standard V. Once a week, groups of girls and boys were marched off in crocodile fashion to the Cookery and Woodwork Centre in the grounds of the Council School.

[There are no prizes for guessing which group learnt what in those sexist days. BUT! Girls were girls and did girlie things whilst boys were boys and did manly things - an arrangement we all enjoyed!]

Girls endured Sewing Lessons whilst the boys were away doing Woodwork. We had to make teeny-weeny stitches on fine hems and French seams and, if Miss Moore could see them with the naked eye, she called them big, ugly dogs' teeth and demanded that they be pulled out and done again. White garments turned ever deeper shades of grey!

Prim Miss Alice Moore aimed for a high standard of behaviour from her pupils. They should be most courteous, well-spoken, quiet in vice and demeanour - proper little ladies in fact. (The latter advice for girls only of course!)

PEGGING RUGS

This was a happy family activity for cold, dark evenings, and provided an excellent opportunity for chats in front of a glowing coal fire. Artistic mothers would draw a geometric pattern on a piece of sacking, which was then stitched tightly on to a wooden frame. All the family sat around it, poking clippings through the sacking, using smooth, wooden 'Prodders' with a pointed end.

Young children's efforts had often to be pulled out after they'd gone to bed.

Visits to Jumble Sales provided plenty of colourful garments, preferably woollen ones, which could be made into clippings measuring about 4in by 1in, with the ends cut diagonally.

Pegged rugs were cosy, warm spots on cold oil-cloth or lino. To keep them looking smart they needed to be well-shaken outside the back door every morning. A new rug would start its life in front of the parlour fireplace, and be moved around the house as it aged: to a bedroom, then the living-room, next to the back-kitchen and eventually it would end its life, worn and ragged, at the foot of the cellar-steps.

JUMBLE SALES

On Friday evenings, Carnforth's working-class women, eager for bargains and a good old chin-wag, headed for the Church Room in Preston Street, a favourite venue for Jumble Sales. Proceedings started at 6pm, but an early arrival was necessary to get good seats near the front. No one wanted to buy pigs in pokes or pants with patches, so it was essential to have a good view of each article as it was held aloft by the auctioneer, a bright chappie with a humorous flow of patter.

Tongues wagged 13 to the dozen during the interval, whilst cups of tea (1d) and fancy cakes (2d) were being served. After the sale, the women went home with bulging bags, happy in the knowledge that they'd had a grand night-out, both socially and economically and some local good-cause had reaped the benefit.

WEATHER FORECASTING

There was no need to consult the newspaper for a weather report. When noses in Carnforth sniffed the strong smell of oil-cloth in production, carried on southern winds from Williamson's factory in Lancaster, folk firmly decided, "It's going to rain."

Eyes were indicators too. When the view of Grange across Morecambe Bay was very clear, that was a sign of rain to come. When Grange couldn't be seen at all, it was raining!

When Aunt Fanny's rheumaticky knee started to "fer gi' 'er gyp", everyone knew that more wet weather was most surely on its way.

A brightly-glowing, crackly coal fire warned that a frosty period was coming, but when it back-draughted and caused smuts to swirl around the room like black snowflakes, strong winds were blowing. Sooty smells puffing down the chimney indicated that Carnforth was cowering under a deep climatic depression.

Coal fires were also capable of fortune-telling. When sooty 'stalactites' swung from the bars of the grate, folk knew they'd better start tidying-up because, for sure, they'd soon have a visit from strangers.

CANNY FARMERS

Good farms abound in our neighbourhood. The soil is light loam overlying gravel, and though much of the land is in pasture, barley, oats and root crops are grown.

Some farmers, who owned land near the railway-line, had a cunning way to acquire free fuel. They stood a scarecrow in a field not far from the track and then waited for a plentiful supply of coal to arrive. As each chuffing train appeared on the scene, the youthful fireman on the footplate took careful aim to hit the poor defenceless scarecrow with a lump of coal as the train steamed by.

BOGGARTS AND GASLIGHT

Children were warned that, if they misbehaved, big, black Boggarts (or their relatives Bogeymen) would come and get them. These scary creatures lurked in bedrooms and back-kitchens where candles did not light-up dark corners, but of course spooky cellars were their favourite haunts.

According to adolescents, Boggarts took their outdoor exercise in gloomy back streets and ginnels during the hours of darkness. This information ensured that, in those areas, sweethearts were safe from inquisitive youngsters.

[When Boggarts left Carnforth, they went to live at Kents Bank near Grange, where today a local hotel

holds Boggart Weekends. If you don't actually meet up with one, there are plenty of replicas on sale to revive your memory, and liquid refreshment helps in the process. There is no need to fear for your safety because modern boggarts are strict vegetarians!]

Many were the happy hours we young children spent playing in the pools of light below Hill Street's gas-lamps. We loved to tie a rope on the cross bars and 'dizzy' around the posts.

The Carnforth Gas Company had a large gasometer situated close to the back of Alexandra Road, making the residents' outlook in that direction very dark and unattractive.

The Company's manager lived at The Gas House, which stood nearby, alongside Lancaster Road, and folk went there to pay their gas bills.

Mr Ellery, whose home was a cottage in Lower North Road near The Council School, was our town Lamplighter. He was a lish, li'l fellow and, like a soldier with a gun, he marched off smartly on his rounds carrying a long pole with a hook at one end.

CULTURE-ISM

"Oh, him! He lives down Dudley, and I'm not sitting next to Him!"

This insulting remark was still made occasionally in Carnforth's two schools, by children whose forefathers considered themselves to be true Carnforthians.

It was over 50 years since whole families had been brought here from the Dudley area of the Black country to work at the Haematite Iron Works, established in 1864, and to live in streets built especially for them in Millhead. Our population in 1851 was only 294, and was made up of people who, for the most part, worked on the land and had no knowledge of industrial labour.

The two communities had still not fully integrated because of their different cultures. 'Dudleyites' thought Carnforthians were reet snooty and, quite without justification, some of the latter declared that Millhead was a rough place where the police had to walk around in pairs!

FRONTS

Advice from a mother to a young Carnforth bride: "Now then our Mary, allus keep thy front nice and clean. Think on! Moo-er fowks walks past thy front doo-er than ever comes in!"

So every Friday, conscientious housewives were down on their knees scrubbing the semi-circular area around their front doors. The edge of the step and all round the coal-hole was donkey-stoned, while the grate was polished with Zeebo till it shone as bright as the armour of a brave knight.

Windows must also have a clean, well-cared for appearance, preferably with an aspidistra smiling out at the world from between clean, white, lace curtains, looped neatly at each side. Blinds at the front of the house were fawn and were pulled down by a crochet-covered marble which dangled from a cord.

Sadly, smart fronts didn't always present a true picture of a home's interior. Some slap-dash women would sail forth early in the day, dressed up to the nines with frizzy bunches of hair at each side of their painted faces. They had done their fronts, but oh dear! The state of their houses indoors! Beds weren't made and had layers of dust under them, pots weren't emptied, cellar-steps were unswept, dirty clothes were piled in a heap in the kitchen, and the closet in the back-yard...? That was a downright disgrace!

AND BACKS

One morning, having been out the back to empty the ashes into the midden, my mother returned indoors with a face like thunder. She'd had a ding-dong with him next-door! The poor chappie had been taken short during the night and, because it was pouring down in torrents, he'd emptied his po into the drain by his back door, which was our drain because of the arrangement of down-spouts from the roof.

"I scrub that drain out on wash-days every week," declared my cross mothers, "and I'm not putting up with filthy tricks like that!"

"Oh dear," said the intimidated neighbour. "It must have been a dog."

"A dog!" shouted my mother. "If dogs round here have started wiping themselves with paper, I can only say most certainly that they have much cleaner habits than people I could name!"

Such a thing never happened again!

NATIONAL NEWS

There was a lot of talk in Carnforth pubs about three national topics reported in the newspapers:

1. Firstly, they were all proud to read that Britain had got its own national airline: Imperial Airways, which had a fleet of 13 aircraft flying from Croydon. Would any Carnforthians ever fly in an aeroplane? Doubts were expressed when, a while later, they heard that 8 people had died in Britain's worst air crash. Better stick to trains!

2. None of the chaps had a car, so did not feel deeply involved on reading that there were discussions in Parliament about introducing tests for drivers. They thought it advisable though, if the tests would cut the number of road accidents. All our town had been saddened when a little girl, called Winnie Keegan, had been killed on her way home from the Roman Catholic church at Bolton-le-Sands.

3. It gave young farm-workers something to consider when they read that the

Government was encouraging 3,000 families to emigrate to Canada and live on farms over there.

ANOTHER CHRISTMAS

Christmas-time was with us again and, with lighted candles in jam-jars, we enjoyed carol-singing, snugly wrapped in big, woolly scarves crossed over our chests and safety-pinned behind our backs. To that household which did not spare us a penny, and where our melodious rendering of 'Hark The Herald Angels' was drowned out by the loud barking of a frenetic bitch, no seasonal greetings to you! We know you hadn't a dog!

Father Christmas braved our sooty chimneys and generously filled our stockings, which were hanging on the rail at the foot of our beds, with an apple, an orange, some nuts, a sugar pig, a bag of gold chocolate coins, a liquorice Smoker's Set and a special toy.

Various branches of family trees squeezed into small living-rooms to enjoy happy Christmas dinners - a goose perhaps, or a rabbit pie.

A Merry Christmas everyone and don't forget the Congs concert tomorrow evening!

1925

As had become practice, all the locomotives in the railway marshalling-yards blew their whistles to welcome in the New Year.

Among the crowd which gathered in the new Garden of Remembrance were grieving families. They were comforted to feel the nearness of the loved ones they had lost in the War as they gazed up at the figure of the soldier with bowed head, which stood on the monument of Carnforth's War Memorial.

CAP THAT!

Money was scarce and many folk were having to watch every penny to make ends meet. At this most inappropriate time some powers-that-be had the foolish idea of introducing uniforms at the two schools. The purchasing of headgear was as far as the matter ever went. At Cobbe's school, the lads' navy-blue caps and the lasses' 'pork-pie' style hats had badges with the red, intertwined initials CCE - Carnforth Church of England. At Barnard's New Council School the badges on the caps and 'Dutch-girl' type hats were the yellow letters CCS - Carnforth Council School.

War was declared between the wearers of those badges. "Cobbe's Clever Elephants" was the battle cry with which they taunted us. In reply we shouted, "Carnforth Cow Sheds," but with little conviction because we knew, but wouldn't admit it, that their school was far superior to ours. They had separate classrooms, an assembly hall, corridors, well-equipped cloakrooms and a Staff Room. Nevertheless we said to ourselves, "A building doth not a School make!"

Battles raged before and after the twice daily sessions at School. After wild chases along Lancaster Road, North Road, Oxford Street, New Street etc., caps were snatched off heads, thrown over walls, stamped on in dusty roads, hurled into people's gardens and tossed into puddles on rainy days.

Gradually the number of caps decreased and parents would not pay for their replacement, so the dream of having Carnforth scholars smartly attired in uniform just faded away.

FOOD FOR THOUGHT

Wives donned clean pinnies to welcome home husbands with wage packets after work on Fridays. Money for food was given top priority, and every penny had to be spent wisely.

Mothers aimed to make meals which would stick to ribs and make hairs grow on the chest - inducements which horrified their daughters!

Not a crumb had to be wasted and the sparrows around our town became and thin and bony. Plates must be cleaned up after every meal. If a child dared to leave a fried egg at breakfast-time, it was served again, staring up like an accusing eye, on the dinner-plate. Still uneaten, it appeared again at the tea-table and at supper-time. In sheer desperation, and with eyes shut tight, the child downed the egg before going to bed.

Rules were adhered to rigidly. A wasted first course meant no second course - "Eat up your cabbage or no pudding", "Leave your bread and butter, then no cake!" Mothers became fiery dragons if noses were snewed up at their thoughtfully prepared meals.

With thrifty planning, the Sunday roast-beef, mutton or pork could last well into the week, being served in cold slices on Monday, cut into chunks for a hot-pot on Tuesday, and minced in a metal contraption, which screwed on to the kitchen table, for a cottage-pie on Wednesday.

Other first courses were fish, stew with dumplings, sheep's-head soup, and various pies preferably with suet crusts: cow-heel, steak-and-kidney or rabbit.

Favourite sweet courses were milk puddings (7d per quart for milk), Spotted Dick, suet roly-poly puds (fruit, jam or syrup) boiled in pieces of cloth - not Grandma's' stocking - stewed rhubarb and baked egg custard. (Suet was used in a lot of dishes. It was bought in large chunks at the butcher's' and grated at home).

The kind of meals served depended largely upon a

family's financial means. The less well-off had dripping on toast for breakfast, whilst more affluent folk enjoyed bacon and egg, fried on their paraffin stoves. Tripe, black-pudding, pigs' trotters, boloney, cockles and mussels, kippers and roll-mop herrings were all tasty tea-time treats.

Tea-times were special on Sundays, starting with ham or salmon salad, and then one of the following - a trifle, fruit pie, slice of cake, jelly and custard, a junket or tinned Bartlett pears topped with Carnforthian milk and served in a glass dish. Très posh.

To have a meal seated around the living-room table, covered with a snowy linen cloth, was an enjoyable social occasion when family news could be exchanged. Grace was said before any food was eaten and no child would move away until it had made the request, "Please may I leave the table?"

HOME CURES

I shared my Barnham grandparents with 13 cousins and, when we visited them, we perched very uncomfortably on their prickly horse-hair sofa and said nowt. "Children," said our granddad, "must be seen and not heard!" We most assuredly would not have mentioned upset tummies, because he would have threatened us with a dose of Indian Brandee from his home-made medicine cabinet, which hung on the living-room wall. That vile, fiery liquid would have burnt a hole in our innards!

Medicines, which were strongly coloured and tasted horrible, did you good psychologically as well as medically. Just thinking about them could cure you!

Every good home in Carnforth had a medicine chest with a plentiful supply of well-tested, family remedies: fiery Sloane's Liniment for aching backs, Camphorated oil for wheezy chests, tins of Zambuk and boracic ointment for cuts and grazes, Iodine to kill infection. Cascara, Turkey rhubarb, senna pods, Beecham's Pills (worth a guinea a box!) and, horror of horrors, castor-oil, were all guaranteed to get awkward bowels on the move.

Burning hot poultices were a powerful cure for boils and abscesses. They could contain either bread or boiled linseed, wrapped in a piece of white rag. Olive-oil was poured from a warmed spoon into painful ears and the patient then went out-of-doors wearing a woolly scarf wrapped around the face and knotted bunny-rabbit style on top of the head. More effective and comforting was a hot potato inside an old sock held to the aching ear. The ingredients for cough-cures could be many - vinegar, butter, glycerine, lemon juice, honey and rum, and were mixed according to one's own preference. Not all home remedies were to be found in a medicine chest however. The cure for chilblains was to dip the painful toe in a po with liquid contents. If you happened to be taking a course of D'Ewett's Kidney Pills, those liquid contents could give you a nasty shock. They were bright green!

As they sat in their desks at school during the winter months, strong odours emanated from some children whose chests had been literally rubbed with goose-grease. All germs in the vicinity dropped dead. During school medical inspections, Dr Tomb and his nurse had difficultly with undressing some children whose fond mothers had neatly stitched them up in red flannel to protect them from biting winds. Around the necks of other kiddies hung little cotton bags full of moth-balls, which would hopefully fight infection.

Realising that prevention is better than cure, most caring mothers gave their brood a tonic such as Scott's Emulsion (ugh!) or Parrishes Chemical Food, reputed to be full of iron and would give you rosy cheeks. One of my aunties was a firm believer in Virol. Most probably it did those cousins of mine a lot of good because their cat, which always licked the spoon, had the glossiest fur of all the felines in Carnforth.

Invalids were soothed with beef tea, oatmeal gruel, calve's foot jelly, Benger's food, slippery elm and pobs (hot milk on bread and sugar). My dad's cure-all was well worth being ill for - Wincarnis!

ESCAPE FROM DRUDGERY

In the cotton towns of Lancashire, many married women were employed in the mills, but in Carnforth it was considered that a woman's place is in the home. Each day brought its round of chores: Monday, washing day; Tuesday, ironing; Wednesday, bed-rooms; Thursday, baking; Friday, the living-room, the front, the back, the closet, the cellar-steps etc. etc. A woman's work was never done!

In April, newspapers made a wonderful announcement: women would soon be freed from the drudgery of housework by machines! Catering establishments, it was reported, already had machines for washing dishes and processing food, and experts predicted that smaller scale versions for ordinary homes were just around the corner.

Until that corner was turned, Carnforth women made their own escape from drudgery by having a Saturday afternoon outing to Lancaster on a local train, calling at Bolton-le-Sands and Hest Bank. My mother and I liked to look round Reddrop's, Studholme's, Lawson's, Tominson's Music Shop and a new sort of store in Penny Street which had goods, costing 3d and 6d, displayed on counters all round the sides of the shop. Its name was Woolworths.

In the Market, I liked to choose an old copy of 'School Friend' for 1d and, at the Toffee Stall, my mother once allowed me to buy a packet of Wrigley's Chewing gum, of which she did not approve, because I said I wanted to solve a puzzle posed by a popular song, "Does your Spearmint lose its flavour on the Bed-post overnight?" (It did.)

We enjoyed hot pies and gravy, seated at a marble-topped table in one of the cubicles at the Coffee Tavern, which had a shiny brass tea-urn steaming away on the counter. After that, we headed off to The Grand Theatre and queued up for the First House to see an amusing revue or any interesting variety show. A supper of fish and chips, tea, bread and butter (9d) was eaten at a chip shop in Nicholas Castle Station. Who could wish for a better outing?

Balmy sea-breezes beckoned us to Morecambe during the warm summer weather. The train from Carnforth travelled there via the single-line track from Hest Bank to Bare Lane. After a stroll along the promenade and a paddle in the pool near the Stone Jerry, we sat on the rocks to enjoy our sandwiches, washed down by tea bought at a nearby stall - 1s 4d per jug, the shilling being refunded when the jug was returned.

In good time, we queued up to pay our 6d admission money to The Winter Gardens. We were not used to luxury and didn't mind sitting 'up in the Gods' on tiered steps of the Upper Gallery, and clapped enthusiastically as the variety artists performed on the stage far down below us. After the show, we could go into the magnificent ballroom and watch crowds of dancers doing the barn dance, waltz, foxtrot, valetta or military two-step to the music of a large dance-band on the stage.

A vinegary parcel of fish and chips from a shop in Euston Road was eaten with relish on the way to the station for the 10pm train home. Crowds of young people travelled on a later train, known mysteriously as the whip, and on that groups of youths from Kendal had playful rough-houses with Carnforth lads.

TALKING POINTS

1. The exciting budget introduced by Winston Churchill in April caused a lot of discussion among Carnforth men. Britain was back on the Gold Standard! The age at which old people received their pensions was reduced from 70 to 65 years. Income tax was down 4 shillings in the £, which meant that a person earning £500 per annum would pay about £19. In a new contributory insurance scheme, men and their employers would pay 4d per week and women 2d.

2. The National Council of Public Morals withheld its approval of contraception, according to the newspapers. Contraception? "Come on you Know-It-Alls," said the lasses at Morphy's Mill. "Tell us what that's all about!" The lasses hoped that, at the next dance in the Co-op Hall, Mrs Penswick at the piano would oblige by pepping up the music, so that they could try out a new dance that had scandalised America. Newspapers reported that 'The Charleston', performed at

a frenetic tempo, was a hit both with débutantes and shop-girls ... and most probably mill-girls too!

3. Should Carnforth people do them, or leave them alone? What had been a nursery game for 100 years had just become a national craze: crossword puzzles! The British Optical Association feared they would cause headaches and eye-strain, but the American verdict was that they give people a mental kick which is good for health and happiness.

4. Farming folk were again being asked to consider emigration. It was said that, over the next 10 years, half a million would be encouraged to leave Britain and make their homes in Australia. They would be taught how to manage and develop new farms, and the Australian Government and the Colonial Office would agree to build roads, bridges and railways, and help settlers to buy stock and equipment. *[Quite a number of Carnforth people joined this scheme and emigrated.]*

5. Local people suffering from Diabetes were glad to hear that a patient at Guy's Hospital had been given the first successful treatment for the complaint.

6. Trade was brisk at the Carnforth Motor Company's premises. New cars were becoming faster (some claiming a top speed of 60 mph!) and cheaper, e.g. £145 for a 3-

seater Citroen or £150 for a 2 cylinder Jowett with a self-starter. How remarkable! No more laborious winding-up of the engine at the front with a starting handle. White lines were to be painted on roads all over Britain in an attempt to reduce accidents, and traffic lights were proposed in Piccadilly Circus, London. A new law was introduced to punish drunken drivers with up to 4 months in gaol, but there was no prison sentence for reckless driving. The problem was the difficulty of telling when a driver was drunk.

NO CHAINS TO PULL!

From the back doors in our shared yard, well-worn pathways led to a small building with 4 doors, behind which were cubicles containing earth closets. Those 'inconveniences' were very effective constipaters.

At the back of the building, which formed the end of our short back-street, was a 2-part door. Through the top part neighbours tossed, not earth, but ashes from their fires, and all their household rubbish. In some areas of Carnforth (not ours!) very mischievous lads had been known to lie in wait for some hapless person to enter his cubicle in answer to a call of Nature. The young rascals then attacked the vulnerable one at the rear with a bunch of nettles attached to a long stick, which they pushed through the half-open door.

Both halves of that midden door were only opened

once a week, when the malodorous contents were raked out and shovelled up into the horse-drawn muck cart by two long-suffering Council workmen, who then poured pink disinfectant all around.

When the cart was fully loaded, Pim the horse was led to the town tip - first turn right over Kellet Road canal bridge. No protective gear whatsoever was issued to those midden men. Not even nose-pegs! Mrs Ashton and Mr Cambray (a couple of Toms) were our neighbours in Hill Street and, in spite of their disgusting jobs, their homes were spotless - a tribute to their hard-working wives!

It was believed that a woman's character could be judged from the condition of the family's earth closet. Ours was immaculate, its frequently white-washed walls cobweb-free.

Every Friday, wearing a hessian apron and a dust-cap, my mother waged war on dirt with a bucket of hot water and a scrubbing brush. Pastry could have been rolled out on that board with a hole in it! Just the one hole in our case, but it was known for some to have two, to accommodate both a lady and gent, and even a small third one for a child.

I often used our closet as a pleasant, mother-free reading-room. Threaded on string and hanging on a hook behind the door were neat squares of paper, coarsely known as bum-fodder. They had been cut from the railway time-books and would have been very boring reading-matter, so I raced across there with a copy of 'Chicks' Own' comic-paper, hidden up one of my knicker-legs. I had to take our long sweeping-brush with me because, on occasions, I had been imprisoned there by Ashton's belligerent banty-cock which led its six faithful wives to peck our backyard grass. That fearsome bunch of brown and gold feathers would fiercely attack any human leg in sight!

Earth closets in our shared backyard (now subdivided). Background: Morphy's Mill with the wall of Rigg's Yard on the right. (photo 1985)

After dark, the trip 'up t'yard' could be very hazardous. Candles invariably blew out and left one in complete blackness. To guide its members across there safely, some families had a clothes-line stretched from their back door to the handle of their closet door. I used to press down the sneck to open ours and then step back smartly, in case an old tramp or a ghost was seated inside.

Folk had to have an urgent need to compel them to go out there in bad weather. An old coat was kept on a hook behind the back kitchen door to throw over one's head as protection from pouring rain. Sitting over there could be a chilling experience and sometimes the paper would keep blowing back out of the hole because of the strong wind.

Flies and bluebottles from all over Lancashire seemed to wing their way to our earth closet and, after sampling its delights, they made explorative flights into our homes through open back-doors. Dozens and dozens of careless ones got a leg or wing entrapped on the sticky surface of a long, yellow fly-paper (1d each at Possie's) where they suffered slow, painful deaths. The more fortunate winged beasties strolled about on any foods which had been left uncovered on the open surfaces of back kitchens or at each side of the cellar steps where food had been placed for coolness.

Like other Carnforth wives, my mother crocheted protective covers for jugs and bottles. Appropriate words such as 'MILK' or 'SUGAR' were cleverly worked into the pattern, and beads were spaced out around the edges to keep the covers weighted down.

Perhaps at some future date, people might consider our sanitary arrangements quite disgusting, but we did not worry unduly about them because we knew of nothing different. As far as we were aware, King George V and the Royal

Family had an Earth Closet outside the back door of Buckingham Palace, but where we had a horse-shoe nailed-up they would be displaying a Royal Coat-of-Arms.

OUR LIQUID ROAD

Behind a stout barrier of big railway sleepers across the bottom of Hill Street was the 57 mile-long Preston to Kendal Canal, which winds for about a mile through our town and is rich in roach, perch, pike and eels.

Before we went out to play, our mothers would say to us, "Now think on! Keep off them banks!" But the water always looked very inviting and, on occasions, we'd yield to Satan's temptation and wriggle through a gap in the fence.

Sometimes we walked along the tow-path as far as the canal-basin opposite Hewthwaite Terrace, and watched the unloading of barges which had come from the Lancashire Coalfield. A lot of the coal shovelled off was loaded into barrows and wheeled into Carnforth Gas Company's Works which, along with the large gas-holder, stood behind Alexandra Road.

From the canal bank, we children looked through an opening in the wall of the boiler-house and gazed down in horror at the frightening scene in the big, gloomy interior. The black figures of workmen showed up in the fierce, fiery glow as they heaved huge shovelfuls of coal through the

Canal Basin and Bank Ranger's Cottage. The Gasworks, its chimney and gas-holder are in the centre.

open furnace doors. Hot sulphur fumes rose up and made us gasp and cough, and hot blasts of air caused us to jump back in alarm.

Those poor men! Stripped to the waist and working down there in such appalling conditions! We felt sure they'd try very hard to live righteous lives so that they'd eventually inherit snowy-white robes and soft, downy wings when they died. They'd already had more than enough of fiery furnaces in nether regions.

Chattering, inquisitive groups of children were not welcomed by anglers, often to be seen spaced out at intervals along the bank of our canal.

Excursion trains brought them from Lancashire's busy mill towns and mining areas to enjoy the tranquillity and beauty of our district, whilst taking part in fishing competitions. We would not have liked to eat any of the fish they caught because there were lots of horrible sacks in the water containing the decomposing bodies of cats and dogs. Drowning them was the accepted method of disposing with unwanted pets. That put girls off swimming in the canal, however hot the weather! Some lads were not so fussy and, to help their families, they swam near the basin and dived down to collect lumps of coal, which had dropped into the water when barges were being unloaded.

We knew we were being naughty when we took off our boots and stocks and had a go at fishing with a worm dangling on a bent pin, suspended on a length of string. Very rarely did such efforts bring success. Minnows were very elusive and not worth getting in trouble for. It was wiser for us to wait until our dads bought us fishing-nets, and took us on the banks carrying jam-jars, with handles of string, into which we could put tiddlers, and those delightful black wiggly commas called tadpoles.

When it froze over in winter, our canal offered a dangerous invitation. My friends and I were out on a sedate walk one day, wearing our Sunday-best attire, when we saw a group of daring children having a hilarious time sliding on the ice. The temptation was too great! I joined them, and richly deserved what happened. Crack! The ice broke and one of my legs plunged into the freezing water. I struggled to safety but one of my smart leather gaiters was ruined - soaking wet and all wrinkled up. I knew my mother would play war with me. She did. I wasn't sorry about the gaiters though, I hated them! Stiff, uncomfortable things they were, and the little button-hook my mother used to fasten them on me pulled a bit of my flesh through the holes along with each button. Ouch! The agony! Good riddance to them!

KIDS

1. Children on their way to and from school were eager to know what was going on in our town. Why were lengths of our roadway being dug up? Why were brown earthenware pipes stacked in inviting piles at intervals alongside the diggings? Didn't the workmen's unattended equipment look interesting? A group of mischievous lads stopped by a big barrel and, climbing on top, Sammy Rucastle, performed a wild Red Indian war dance. His triumphant whoops stopped dramatically as the cover became dislodged and plunged him into the contents ... black sticky tar!

He was not given a loving welcome by his mother when he arrived in floods of tears at his home in Haws Hill.

A sewerage scheme costing £1,300 was in progress for Cragbank.

2. A little gang from Hill Street would sometimes set out to explore the play-potential of our surrounding area. There was piece of spare land

alongside Lancaster Road [where the library now stands], but Robin Bagguley and the other King Street children ruled over that. Quite close by, Robinsons, the Nether Kellet builders, had dug the foundations for five new houses (numbers 1A to 5A Alexandra Road) and they were a very interesting place to play if the local children would tolerate us. Of course it was nice and exciting if they picked a chase-you-away fight with us.

3. "The Lake District" was the derisive name which the rest of Carnforth gave to Hunter Street, Ramsden Street, Pond Street and Pond Terrace, because of the proximity of a pond which, at one time, had been a cooling reservoir for the Iron Works. Pipes had been laid in both directions under the railway lines to connect the pond and the Works.

That district had a powerful street gang, which drove off intruders from other areas. Some of the leaders belonged to a family of 11 children (7 boys) called Russell who lived at 7 Ramsden Street. Naturally the games of that district centred mostly around the pond, on which they sailed, balancing precariously on home-made rafts.

A little boy from Barrow used to stay with Mrs Graham in Hunter Street and, when she wanted to summon him in from play, she did not shout his name from the doorway as most mothers did; she blew a whistle to which he was expected to respond immediately.

If the summons came when he was on a raft in the middle of the pond, he instantly stepped off into the water and waded ashore. There was prompt obedience for you!

4. Kids, whose parents could not afford to give them a Saturday penny, found that by being polite, pleasant and respectful to their 'elders and betters' they could always earn themselves some pocket-money. Housebound people were glad of a trustworthy child to run errands for them.

Lads found that a homemade bogcy (four old pram wheels on a wooden box from the Co-op) could be a money-spinner, when used for transporting loads of various commodities: coke from the gas-works, firewood from the wood-yard, freshly-gathered 'coddies' to backyard gardens etc.

It was expedient to watch for Mr Weeks, newsagent and Kinema Manager, to emerge from his shop with a bundle of envelopes in his hand. A polite, "Please sir, may I go to the Post Office with your mail?" could earn them free admission to a matinee at the pictures, and perhaps a job as a paper-boy.

On occasions, it could be profitable to hang about the Auction Mart area. Farmers might reward the lads with a copper if they offered to help drive animals down Market Street and along Warton Road to the pens in the railway goods yard.

5. The Drill Hall, used by the 5th King's Own

Regiment, was situated at the corner of Station Buildings, with its entrance at the top of Hunter Street. It occupied the 1st floor and below it was a shop, which often had an inviting open sack of monkey nuts outside its door.

Boys with out-stretched arms made loud buzzing noises as they flew like aeroplanes all around the area. Occasionally they dipped a wing as they swooped around the shop corner, and scooped up a few nuts out of the sack as they zoomed past. Naughty aeroplanes!

GOING' TUT PITCHERS

A seat at the Kinema could transport folks from the grim reality of their every day lives to Fantasy Land: the wonderfully rich world of Tinsel Town (Hollywood), where exquisitely dressed people lounged about in luxurious surroundings. The warmth, the darkness and the comfy seats at the Kinema were very relaxing. Our picture-house was not in the 'laugh and scratch' category! People in the many-surrounding villages were envious of our imposing building and came in bus-loads to share in its delights.

The uniformed usherette, who paraded the aisle with her torch, obligingly did not shine its beam on Sloppy Annas who were enjoying a canoodle on the back row. Sometimes, youths who had paid only 3d to sit in the seats at the front, wriggled under the rows to sit in the 6d seats farther back. Their excuse was that the nearness of the screen had given them embarrassing views up the film star's clothes, and had caused them to have painful kinks in their necks.

Everybody smoked, and the beams from the projection room at the back had a difficult job forcing their way to the screen through thick clouds of cigarette smoke.

In the darkness, the clever pianist chose music to create the appropriate atmosphere for the storylines of the films: a plaintive tune for a heart-rending scene of a harsh father casting-out his erring daughter into the deep, deep snow, with her innocent babe clutched to her breast, loud thumpy music for villainous deeds, and prancy tunes for the skirmishes of Cowboys and Indians on horse-back.

Our films were Movies, a wonderful step in progress from the days of lantern-slides, but they were silent. The film characters opened and shut their mouths but nowt was heard! The dialogue came up on screen in printed form and you needed to be a good, quick reader to keep up with the plot.

The National Anthem was played at the end of each programme and everyone stood to attention and sang with patriotic fervour.

Each Saturday afternoon at 2pm, crowds of us children flocked to the 'Tuppenny Rush'. We were a boisterous audience, clapping and cheering for the goodies and hissing and booing the baddies, whose villainous leader was recognised by his black hat and his moustache, which curled up at the ends.

Cowboys and Indians were our favourites, but we had to be able to move our heads quickly to avoid flying arrows. The 'kissy bits' in films were greeted with titters and hoots of derision.

During the interval song, music came up on the screen and we all sang with gusto as a little white ball bounced merrily from word to word. The songs we liked best were, "Horsy, keep your tail up", "Yes, we have no bananas", "Ever so goosey-goosey-goo", and "The Sheikh of Araby" (at the end of each line we shouted very saucily: "Without a shirt!")

After each performance, we went through the emergency side-door, and sometimes boys slipped around to the back of the building and rooted about among the piles of sweepings-up to try to find two matching torn halves of admission tickets with which they could trick their way into an evening programme.

Once I searched there too and found lots and lots of buttons, which I washed, threaded on to a length of string and gave to my mother as a birthday present. She spent a lot of time sewing.

The Kinema was our first form of canned entertainment and we loved it!

OAK APPLE DAY

On a certain morning in May, most of us arrived in the school-yard wearing a bunch of oak leaves pinned to our clothing. Just before the bell was rung to summon us into straight lines, ready to be marched upstairs to our classrooms, we stamped around the yard, chanting at the top of our voices so that our teachers would hear:

"Oak Bob Day,
The 29th of May,
If you don't give us a holiday,
We'll all run away."

They didn't! And we didn't! At playtime though, there was a real rough-and-tumble as children not wearing oak leaves were chased by toughies, who tried to sting them with nettles (brought to school in newspaper parcels).

There was a great deal of shouting and screaming, which was much enjoyed. The wise amongst us had our pockets stuffed with dock leaves, which could take the pain out of smarting nettle strings.

Probably Oak Apple Day did little to help our historical knowledge about King Charles II, who hid in a leafy oak tree to escape from Oliver Cromwell's Roundheads. They had defeated his Cavaliers at the Battle of Worcester in 1651. May 29th was the King's birthday so that date had been chosen to celebrate his escape. The event, however, did give us some help with our Botany lessons. We could all recognise the wavy outline of an oak leaf!

CARNFORTH'S DEAD CENTRE CONSECRATED

An important event took place in June - our town acquired its first burial ground.

In front of Russell Road and alongside Kellet Road were two adjacent fields, separated by a stream which flooded during heavy rain, causing the water to reach the height of downstairs windows sills in Russell Road on occasions. Mr Adamson (the Barber and Tobacconist) kept some pigs and hens in the first field. It was the field beyond that which had been chosen as the cemetery.

Dignitaries from our churches and members of the Council were present when, after a short service, the beautiful, big wrought-iron gates were opened for the first time. From that time on, it was no long necessary for funerals to make that sad, slow journey to Warton Churchyard.

A GRAND TRIP

By holding Whist Drives, Dances, raffles etc. during the winter months, the Committee of the National Deposit Friendly Society had raised over £20 to give the children of its 300 members a summer outing.

On the great day, according to an article in The Lancaster Guardian, 100 children and 50 adults set off for Grange-over-Sands in 5 coaches, each prominently proclaiming the fact that it was

Carnforth NDFS on an outing - a good form of propaganda!

"Attendance at a picture-show was followed by a splendid tea. Then, as the weather behaved badly, games, singing and recitations helped to make up a pleasant time." It was the intention of the club to make this an annual affair.

[Did £20 pay for all this?]

BY THE FIRESIDE

The fireside was the heart of the home. It was the spot where, when the wind was whiffling down the chimney, parents could relax after work in the comforting warmth of a cracking coal fire, with its flickering flames making fascinating ever-changing patterns.

Mothers then felt rewarded for the whole of an hour on their knees every Friday, busy with Zeebo for the grate's iron-work and Brasso for the fire-irons (kept like shining gold and too artistic to use!), which were neatly arranged on the enamelled metal hearth-plate with its surrounding brass fender.

The shelf over the fire-grate was known as the Mantelpiece and, from it, posh people liked to hang a red chenille pelmet with wobbly bobbles. Less affluent folk preferred to have a piece of string stretched across so that wet towels and socks could dry-off there.

Nearly every home had a mirror hanging from a nail knocked into the wall over the fireplace - a dangerous fire hazard!

An assortment of odds and ends was kept ready to hand at one end of the mantelpiece, which fortunately was high enough to be out of the reach of inquisitive young fingers: mother's spectacles, dad's pipe, a box of matches, a pair of scissors, a container full of tapers or home-made spills, some unanswered letters awaiting pen and bottle of ink, the money and book "fer t'rent fella", and a collection of club cards (NDFS, Sons of Temperance, the Tontine, Rechabites and so on). Some of the family's precious possessions were displayed up there for safety. A black marble clock often formed the centre-piece and was flanked by a pair of brass candlesticks, a couple of Staffordshire pot dogs and perhaps a pair of velvet-covered photo frames from which the grand-parents stared with stony expressions.

On the wall at one side of the fire-place hung a big pincushion, to ensure that a stitch in time would save nine. From a nail at the opposite side, a pair of bellows was suspended, ready to blow life into the fire if it showed signs of dying. The peaceful scene was disturbed when a volunteer had to clatter down the cellar-steps to bring up a shovelful of coal "fray t'pile under t'coal-'oyl".

CARNFORTH EVENTS

THE CO-OP

1. Members eagerly awaited Dividend Day, and were ready to charge upstairs to the Secretary's Office as soon as the big doors in New Street were opened. They were very thankful to receive their 'divvi' - 2s 6d (hopefully!) returned to them for every £ they had spent at the Society's 6 busy shops in our town. It would come to a considerable amount, and made them feel financially 'flush'. However, they did not dash off to Mrs Helliwell's high-class shop in Market Street to buy themselves a stunning new hat. Indeed not! They were eager to buy new clothes and footwear for their growing children, and necessities for their homes.

2. The Society cannily organised Big Sales at its departmental shops to coincide with Dividend Day - and thus recouped a lot of the money it had paid out! The Co-op Hall was used for a mammoth sale of drapery goods and the event attracted crowds from the surrounding villages.

3. Members' Co-op check-numbers were engraved in their memories for life! My parents' number was 2014 and my Wilkinson and Barnham grandparents' were 52 and 789 respectively.

4. Butter arrived at Carnforth's grocery shops in big wooden barrels. At the marble-topped counter in the Co-op's large shop in New Street, Jim Cooper expertly used butter-pats to shape 1lb and ½lb blocks, which were then wrapped in grease-proof paper. Poor people bought margarine, disparagingly known as Maggie Ann.

   Nearby on the counter, stood a clever bacon slicer operated by a wheel. Customers chose which bacon they wanted from a wide selection of rolls on display, and young Bill Cooper would cut slices of the required thickness.

OTHER MATTERS

1. Dr Edward Jackson had joined his father's practice when he qualified. Young Doctor Eddie, as he became known, married an American lady, and their first home was 28 Market Street, next door to Colbeck's the Chemist. The young wife startled our populace with a very un-English habit. Every morning she opened wide the front bedroom window and draped all the bedding over the sill to air. "Whatever next?" tut-tutted the locals. Didn't foreign folk have funny ways?

2. Crowds flocked to a huge fire at Graveson's Sawmill and Woodyard - just over the Keer Bridge at Millhead. The cost of the damage done was enormous: £3,000!

3. Our hens slowed down their production of eggs as Autumn approached. Like squirrels, wise women prepared for the eventual shortage. They preserved bucketfuls of eggs, either in a lime solution, or in isinglass - bladder of sturgeon. Ugh!

4. The Furness Railway shed was closed down - an event which saddened many railway hearts.

5. Almost every household in Carnforth washed-up with identical, loosely-woven dish-cloths. Could that have been because they were issued to railway employees for all cleaning purposes?

6. A smart brick building was erected on the land behind the War Memorial. It was a Mortuary to replace the shabby old black hut in which Council equipment had been stored - along with unidentified dead bodies!

7. Our town's two Temperance Hotels. 4, Scotland Road and 11 Lower New Street were still providing accommodation safe from The Demon Drink.

8. Because of the lack of space in their Iron Works room, the Mission Church booked the Co-op Hall for their Harvest Festival. A bounteous display of fruit and vegetables filled not only the window ledges, but also a long table in front of the stage, where the

centre-piece was an enormous sheaf of corn made of bread, which had been baked by Jackson's Café at their bake-house in Preston Street. Crowds which packed the forms in the hall and filled the balcony raised the roof with Harvest hymns. It was not only the harmonious sound of a male-voice quartet from Carlisle which delighted the congregation - they were fascinated with the bass singer's active Adam's apple which bobbed up and down in his extremely long neck like an entrapped animal. *[What unlikely events our memories retain?]*

THE FINAL FAREWELL

In the bedrooms of many grandparents, the bottom drawer of the dressing table was reserved for a very special set of beautifully-made white garments: a fine night-shirt, a lovely night-dress, carefully tucked and feather-stitched, and two pairs of very long, white, hand-knitted stockings - laying-out garments ready for the day when the old folk would depart from this world!

REMEMBER, REMEMBER THE 5TH OF NOVEMBER

The highlight of the year was a season rather than a night! During the preceding weeks, gangs of children from various streets had been busily foraging about for sufficient material to build the biggest bonfire in Carnforth.

Firm bonds of team-spirit were formed as large broken branches were dragged from nearby lanes, and parents were pestered for old oilcloth, ragged pegged rugs, sagging mattresses, broken furniture etc.

Like crows in treetops noisily snatching twigs from each others' nests, marauding gangs of children would steal from each other's bonfires, so they needed to be closely guarded.

The Lake District group were very lucky to have Mrs Smith, who would sit on a stool near her doorway with arms folded and a fierce expression on her face, which could scare raiders away from the area.

They were also fortunate to have bonfire material delivered to them by Dockray's cart, just because the horse was stabled behind Hunter Street.

It was comforting to belong to a caring community where everyone would 'muck-in' together to make occasions very special. Mothers were 'reet champion!' They made our Hill Street gang a stuffed man, mysteriously named 'Guy Forks', and dressed him in an old railway uniform. He had to be burnt, so he must have done something bad - driven a train past a signal at red, perhaps? We paraded him about in an old pram and generous folk donated pennies, which our mothers spent on ingredients for clarty gingerbread and sticky toffee.

Muffled up in big woolly scarves safety-pinned at

the back, we dashed off as soon as it was dark to join the crowd gathering around our bonfire. Helpful dads poured paraffin on to it and soon it was well alight. When they poked it with clothes-props, huge flames leapt up into the dark sky and engulfed poor Guy in his wicker chair. Excited faces glowed in the firelight, and delighted oohs and aahs greeted coloured rockets as they whooshed off to the stars. In the whole of Carnforth, our sparklers were the twinkliest, our spinning wheels the whirliest, our Jumping Jacks the leapiest, our Golden Rain the most brilliant, our bangers the most ear-splitting, and our potatoes, baked in the glowing embers, were the most deliciously smoke-flavoured.

Yes, with a doubt, Hill Street bonfire was the best in our town!

A SAD OCCASION

On Sunday November 8th at 3pm, the Second Bronze Panel on the War Memorial was unveiled by the Chairman of the Council, John Murray JP.

During the singing of hymns by the assembled crowd, relatives of fallen soldiers and sailors placed wreaths at the base of the memorial.

The names of the following 10 men, who had died through the effect of their war service, were engraved on the panel: *Bert Cambray, Thomas Cornthwaite, John Nutall, John Parkinson, Victor Postlethwaite, Edward Smith, Richard Smith, Robert*

YOUTHFUL EVENTS

C of E School Football team (1929). In the girls' playground. Steele's woodyard is in the background, separated from school by a 'snicket' known as School Lane (from Lancaster Road to Haws Hill).
Back row (left to right): (1) Arthur Boat (2) Bob Jollys (3) Tom Rawlinson (4) Sam Rucastle (5) Bill Fawcett.
Middle row: (1) Jim Russell (2) Robert Jackson (3) Bill Baines (4) Stan Townson.
Front row: (1) Jack Astley (2) Douglas Dowthwaite.

1. The lad loved football, but he was not allowed to play in the school team because clogs were his only footwear. To overcome the problem, he accompanied his mother to a Jumble Sale and bought an old pair of ladies' button up boots, which he cut in half at ankle-level. He was soon the star of the team! Headmaster Cobbe could not bear his school team to be beaten. If it

looked probable that they were not going to be the winners in a match with a village school in our area, he would blow his whistle on some pretext or other, and march his boys back on the long trek to Carnforth.

2. The Co-op Education Committee had organised a course of elocution lessons for members' children. "I'll tell you what," said Mrs So-and-So to her neighbour. "Them Co-op classes are a washout. Our li'l Lizzie still swears!"

3. Mr Murray, from the taxidermist's shop on Scotland Road, gave the Lake District gang an unusual contribution to their bonfire pile: a moth-eaten but still ferocious-looking stuffed fox. They decided it was too interesting to burn, and planned a new, naughty game for dark nights. They stood that fox on the doorsteps of people who didn't like children, knocked and then ran off to hide, peeping out just in time to see the horrified expression of the person who opened the door and saw the cruel snarling wild animal about to pounce on them.

4. Children loved to spend an evening at the Band of Love, organised by the Salvation Army at the Preston Street Citadel. A big iron stove stood in the middle of the room and the young ones liked to sit close enough to shoot spit balls, which fizzled excitedly as they raced across its fiercely-hot top. As well as warming hearts with lovely stories about Jesus, the Salvation Army

ladies served the children with basins full of delicious pea-and-ham soup to warm their bodies. The helpful lady who boiled the bones at her home had very poor eye-sight and often did not see the bits of paper still adhering to them. Not to worry! Paper isn't poisonous. In fact it might provide extra protein to a bowl of soup.

5. Children became 'Young Britons' when they joined an interesting club held in the Church Room (also in Preston Street). Arts and Crafts were taught there, along with propaganda for the Tory Party. There was an unexpected snag to joining however. Miss Alice Moore, who taught Standard V at our school, was one of the instructors. We children firmly believed that classrooms were the only places for teachers. It was most unsettling to find them intruding in some other sphere of our lives.

6. Mr Strangeways, who had a grey, droopy moustache, was not expected to appear anywhere else but in our Standard VI classroom. Because I was being very talkative one day, he made me stand behind the big blackboard, which could be slid up and down in its heavy wooden stand. When I bent down and continued my conversation with Florence Greenwood he shouted, "Get home girl! I've had enough of you!" Fortunately it was nearly dinner-time so my mother did not know I was in disgrace, and I certainly dare not tell her!

Any complaints to mothers about cross teachers only meant more punishment. Parents and teachers were always on the same side against naughty children!

FOND FAREWELLS

As 1925 drew to its close, two major events were soon to change completely the pattern of my childhood. The first was be the sad parting from my dear Hill Street playmates when our little family moved to 31 Haws Hill, which my parents had bought in 1919.

My Wilkinson grandparents had lived in it since then, having had to vacate their railway house in Grosvenor Place when Granddad reached the retirement age of 70.

To follow next was the loss of my friends at our barn-like C of E School. Moving to the Lancaster Girls' Grammar School in a smart uniform was to cause a great upheaval in my life.

I was astounded to find it even more posh than the Council School! It had separate classrooms, lots of corridors, which had to be walked along sedately and silently in indoor slippers, a big assembly hall, a staffroom, a dining-room, a kitchen, a cookery room, a laboratory, an art room (hurrah!) and a gym (hurrah again!). There were even more places to cheer about: wash-rooms, indoor lavatories (with chains to pull!), a garden, a hockey field, a netball pitch and tennis courts. What a wonderful

The author, photographed in 1985 on the steps of "Granddad Barnham's Signal Box", where he worked from 1885 to 1933. This was reached by a gate in Warton Road, opposite the junction with Keer Road.

new environment I was going to enter!

There were drawbacks in store however: the 8.10am train to Lancaster to catch each morning, a leather satchel in which to carry homework (oh dear!) and end of term reports not only about one's academic achievements, but also about one's conduct (oh calamity!). And what would be missing in this quiet, ladylike school? Boys!

[At this stage in my life, the links in the chain which have always bound me to Carnforth were weakened for a while. 'Ere long they were to tighten again and have strengthened as the years have rolled by.]

GOOD OLD CARNFORTH!

MIND-BLOWING!

As children, our parents had no understanding of the words listed below (nor had we!)

A. Aeroplanes - Anoraks - Acid Rain - Aerobics - Aids - Aliens - Avocados - Antibiotics - Anorexia - Atomic Energy.

B. Bidets - Biros - Baked Beans - Bingo - Bulimia - Bikinis - Burgers - Bungy-jumping - Barbecues.

C. Crisps - Cars - Conkers - Condoms - Calculators - Credit Cards - Canned Custard - Crematoriums - Carers - Cosmonauts - Cameras - Cats Eyes - Contraception - Central Heating.

D. Duvets - Discos - Denim - Double Glazing - Diets - Dole - Drugs - Dust-bins - Dinosaurs - Dyslexia - Dish-washers.

E. E-Mail - Electricity.

F. Family Planning - Fibre-optics - Frozen Foods - Fridges and Freezers - Family Allowance - Fork-lift Trucks.

G. Glue Sniffers - Global Warming - Grapefruit.

H. Helicopters - Hot Dogs - Holidays (abroad) -
Hire-purchase - Hydrogen bombs.

I. Injections - Income Tax - Instant Coffee -
Income Support.

J. Judo - Junk foods - Jogging - Jacuzzis.

K. Keyhole surgery - Karaoke.

L. LSD - Lap-tops - Lottery.

M. Mortgages - Mortuaries - Motor-ways -
Micro-wave ovens - Mobile phones - Moon
landings.

N. Nylon - Nuclear energy.

O. On-line.

P. Passion fruit - Pop music.

Q. Q-tips.

R. Robots - Refugees - Rockets.

S. Sliced bread - Skiing - Soaps (the TV variety)
- Showers - Shorts - Stair-lifts - Space-men -
Snooker - Supermarkets - Soft-ware - Self-
service.

T. TV - Telephones - Track-suits and Trainers -
Tape-recorders - Toaster - Time-shares -
Tights - Transplants - Tea-bags - Tumbler

driers.

U. Uni-sex.

V. Vacuum cleaners - Viagra - Vaccines - Videos
    - Viruses.

W. Washing-machines - Websites - Walkmans.

X. Xerox-machines - X-ray machines

Y. Yoghurt - Yomping - Yoga.

Z. Zimmer frames.

**WHAT CHANGING TIMES WE HAVE LIVED
THROUGH!**

ACKNOWLEDGEMENTS

I want to say a big *Thank You* to the following people who gave or loaned me photographs:

Mrs A Garforth (née Rainford), who now lives in Radcliffe, and has been my friend for 80 years.

Mrs K Barnham of Nelson. My cousin Arthur's widow.

Mrs M Salisbury, my cousin who lives in Alexandra Road.

Mr F Conway, an old Carnforthian now living in Derby.

Mr T Stockton, now living in Lancaster.

Mrs B Watson, Carnforth born and bred!

If you have enjoyed this book, please consider reviewing
it on Amazon or Goodreads (or both)

And feel free visit the Lundarien Press website for more
titles by Marion Russell and other authors:

www.lundarienpress.com

www.ingramcontent.com/pod-product-compliance
Lightning Source LLC
Chambersburg PA
CBHW051047050726
47592CB00002B/429